Physical Education Fireworks!

Fun Games and Activities for "Children of All Ages!"

By Jane Doss

Illustrated by Pat McNeill

Great Activities Publishing Company
Durham, North Carolina

A publication of
The Great Activities Publishing Company
PO Box 51158
Durham, North Carolina
27717-1158

ISBN: 0-945872-12-7

Cover design: Rick Gimlin

Table of Contents

Listing of Activities

Listing of Activities

Dedicated To

I dedicate this book to my family.

My husband Jim
And our sons: Jamie, Jerry and Jeffrey.

For the many years of love, support and understanding.
For endorsing my efforts to balance motherhood and a career.
For helping me to reach for the stars, spread my wings and fly,
and fully enjoy the game of living.

Love and Appreciation,

"Janie Bird"
Jane Buskill Doss

About the Illustrator

Pat McNeill, also known as "Tickie," has taught art for 41 years. She teaches art appreciation and other courses in Continuing Education for Robeson Community College in Lumberton, North Carolina. Her "pride and joy" comes from teaching private art lessons to younger students. Tickie is involved in the local Arts Council and the Christian Care Community Center for seniors.

Prior to moving to North Carolina, she was an art teacher in New York and in San Miguel de Allende, Mexico. Generous with her time and talents, she and Jane Doss became friends while on the staff of a children's summer camp in Massachusetts over 30 years ago.

1

Acknowledgements:

The assistance and services provided by the following friends deserve a heartfelt "Thank you." Their expertise, time invested and willing spirits have contributed more than I can adequately express. They are generous, patient, cooperative, caring and talented. Much of the credit for the successful completion of this book belongs to them.

Jo Higgins and Marilyn Montgomery, volunteer advisors who read and reacted to the manuscript.

Mairo Akpose, a Berry College student worker, who transcribed the manuscript.

Pat McNeill, artist, who spent countless hours illustrating the games and activities.

Jackie Anglin and Kathy Gann, experts in Berry College's Research Lab, who helped and made possible the services of their department.

Artie Kamiya, publisher, who had faith that this book would become a reality as he guided, encouraged and edited this book.

Special Thanks:

I would like to extend special thanks to the folks from Project Adventure and the original New Games Foundation. They have been instrumental in the promotion of cooperative games such as "Smoug's Jewels," "Tennis Ball Frantic," "Hunker Down," and "Ultimate Frisbee." In addition, I would like to thank Terry Orlick for his work in creating, collecting, and sharing games such as "Fish Gobbler," "Sticky Popcorn," and "Blizzard."

- Project Adventure
  PO Box 100
  Hamilton, Massachusetts 01936 (508) 468-7981

- New Games (This is off-shoot of the original New Games Foundation)
  PO Box 1641
  Mendocino, California 95460 (707) 937-3337

- The Cooperative Sports & Games Book by Terry Orlick is published by Pantheon Books, New York.

1 Fun Ice Breakers:
"Starting Off With a Bang!"

For the Physical Education Teacher: We all know how important "first impressions" are. Beginning your class with several cooperative and fun activities can set the stage for the rest of the day or class period. Whether a class is just entering a gym or going out on the playground, it is wise to have some type of game or activity for immediate participation. If you are working with children, teenagers, or adults, a fun warm-up activity is a positive way to get the participants immediately involved. If done on a regular basis thoughout the school year, it creates an image of eager anticipation, provides for minimum "dead time," and causes fewer instances of class disruptions.

For the Classroom Teacher, Recreation Leader, Camp Counselor, or Church Youth Worker: For those working in a school, camp, church, or recreational setting, the games and activities in this chapter can also be very useful! Perhaps you have experienced a feeling of bashfulness or restlessness upon arriving at a social function (dance, party, etc.) where nothing much is going on. Some people might be standing in groups talking or eating, and you have the feeling that you wish you had waited a bit longer before arriving. It is good to begin with an activity the moment the first person arrives so that these negative feelings never happen. This can be accomplished by using proven "activity boosters" or other "pre-party games."

Author's Note:

For Children of All Ages: During my professional career as a college professor, I have worked with groups of all ages (elementary students, teenagers, adults, and seniors) in a variety of settings (school, recreational, and church). While the major purpose of this book is to provide fun and wholesome games and activities for elementary-aged school children, I feel the games in this book can also be used in other settings and with older participants. For example, many of these activities can be used with teenagers in a church or camp setting. The games are also appropriate for multi-generational activities where children, teens, and adults are present!

To help you see these other possibilities, you will see additional age spans listed under the "Age Appeal" headings of each game. This denotes games that have a wide appeal to "children of all ages!"

Jane Doss

Action Reading #1: Clap-Stomp Language

Age Appeal: Grades K-6

Purpose: Perceptual-motor skills

Equipment: "Clap and Stomp"
sheet made into an overhead

Overhead projector and screen

Group Size: Any size

Setting: Gym or classroom

Great for a "Rainy Day"

DESCRIPTION: This is a great activity that can be used in a variety of situations. It can be used to begin a class or as a "settle-down" activity at the end of your class. Using the "Clap and Stomp" sheet, create an overhead or draw the pictures on a large poster. On a signal from the leader, the group reads and acts out actions in sequence and in unison as seen on overhead. For example, the picture with two hands clapping tells the students to clap once. The picture with a foot stomping indicates that the students stomp a foot once, and so on.

> **Teacher Tip:** If the group does not respond in unison, stop and begin again.

Have the students read the "Clap and Stomp" several times. You can suggest a slower tempo, then a faster tempo. Once your students are successful in "reading" the passage, divide the class into two groups. The first group will be responsible for reading the claps. The other group reads the stomps. You can establish your own tempo to match the age of your student (younger students will do better if the tempo is slow and steady).

Variations:
- You can also play a song with a steady 4/4 beat and challenge the group to perform the actions to the music.

- Another variation: As the actions are performed, have the participants change body positions each time.

Clap and Stomp

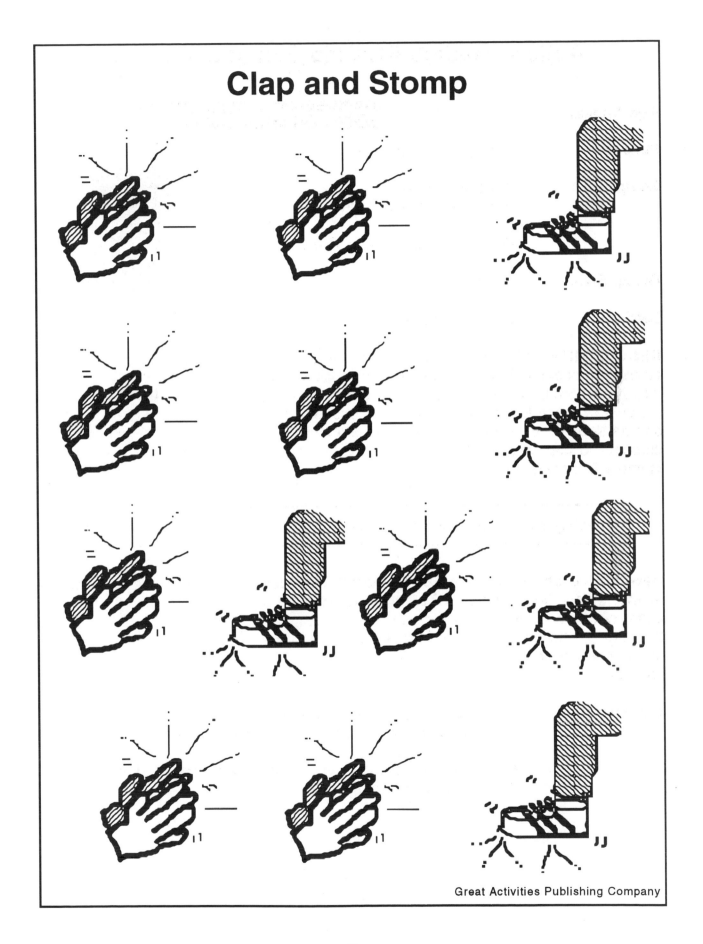

More Action Readings

Age Appeal:	Grades K-6

Also good for teens and adults

Purpose: Perceptual-motor skills, as well as group problem-solving and cooperation

Equipment: Action Reading sheets made into overheads

Overhead projector and screen

Group Size: Any size

Setting: Gym or classroom

Great for a "Rainy Day"

DESCRIPTION: One overhead is shown at a time as the group performs the actions pictured. If group members do not react in unison, they should begin again before moving on to the next card. As the group progresses, they should improve, and can read and react at a faster rate.

The teacher may suggest vocal responses, such as: the picture of a baby would call for a crying sound and the picture of a pig would logically cause the group to say "oink." (However, the teacher could suggest snorting more like a real pig!)

To bring closure to this activity, ask the students to comment on the purpose and value of this activity. Depending on the ages of your students or participants, you may receive responses such as: "it was hard at first," "working together," "makes you laugh a lot," "fosters cooperation," or "helps us practice with patterning and rhythmic beats."

Teacher Tips:

- This activity works well in a setting when some participants arrive late, such as at the beginning of a class when you are waiting for other students to arrive. The students can join in immediately upon arrival. Activities such as this, if done during the beginning of each class, really motivate the students to arrive on time!

- This activity, when used with adults during an Open House or PTA/PTO meeting, gives adults further insight as to what a child learning to read might experience.

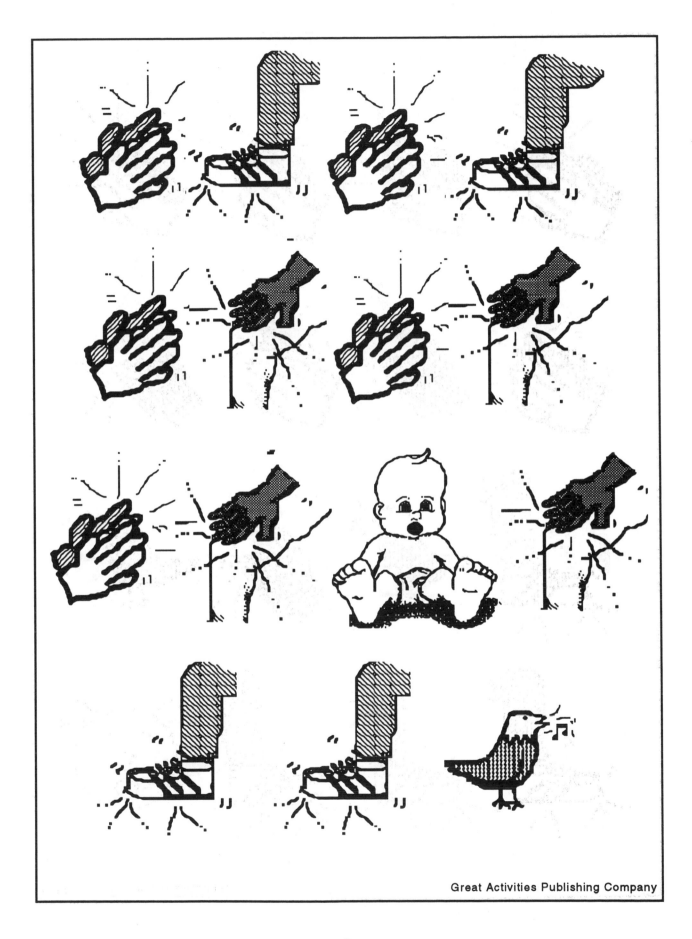

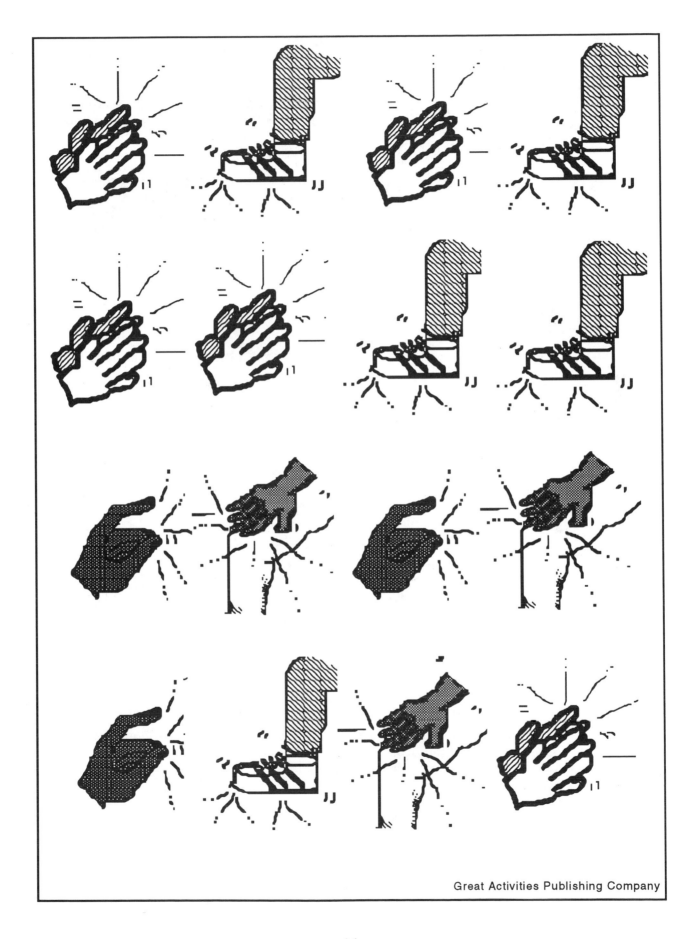

What's Your Physical Education I.Q.?

Age Appeal: Third Grade and Up   **Also good for teens, adults, and seniors**

Purpose: Creative thinking and problem-solving skills

Equipment: Copies of "Physical Education I.Q." sheets for participants

    Pencils

Group Size: Any size

Setting: Gym or classroom

Great for a "Rainy Day"

DESCRIPTION: Divide the class into small groups of 2-3 students. Distribute a copy of the "Physical Education I.Q." sheet to each group. The sheets contain word-pictures of physical education and sports terms. For example, a picture of a house with legs that appears to be running would be "home run." Give your students 3-5 minutes to solve as many of the word-pictures as possible.

When time is up, give the students the correct answers. If time permits, challenge the students to think of their own word-picture on a given topic or a topic of their choice. Each group is given time to draw the word-picture on the back of the sheet of paper. Here are a few examples of possible word-pictures:

- Rhode Island (picture of an island with a road on it)

- Fireman (picture of a campfire and a man)

Variations:
- Design a set of large word-picture cards. The cards can be held up one at a time by the teacher for the students to call out the answers. Or each card can be taped to the walls around the gym or classroom. The object is for the participants to discover a title for each picture and to write the names of the numbered cards on a sheet of paper. After a set time limit, all of the students sit down as the teacher gives the answers.

Can You Guess These Physical Education Terms?

#1

#2

#3

#4

#5

#6

#7

#8

#9

13

Can You Guess These Physical Education Terms?

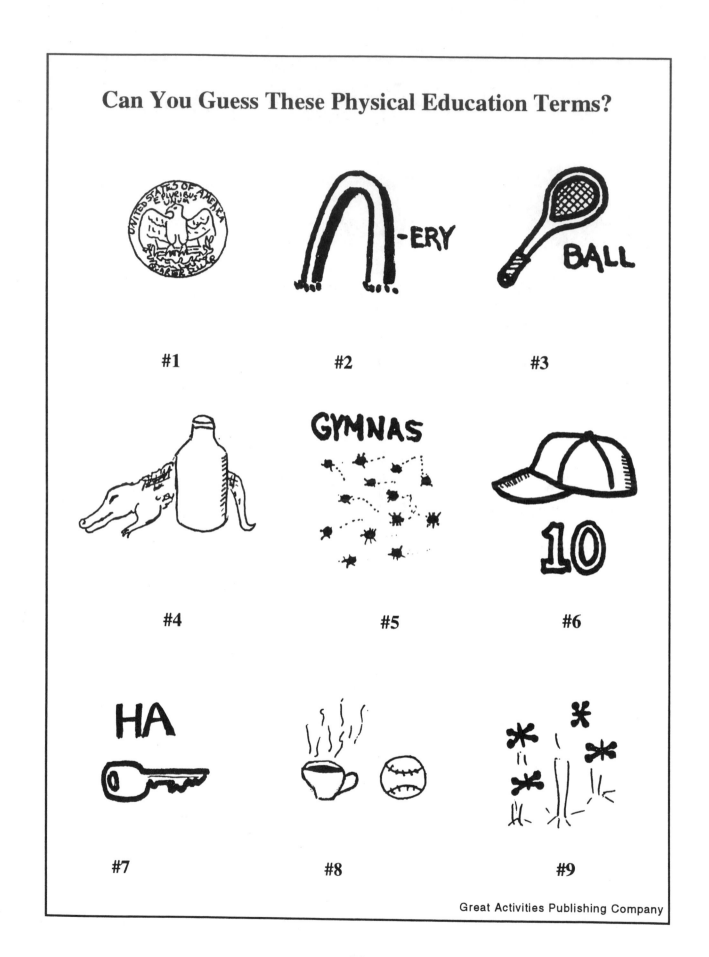

#1

#2 -ERY

#3 BALL

#4

#5 GYMNAS

#6 10

#7 HA

#8

#9

14

Physical Education I.Q. Test
Answers

Page 13

#1: Hole in One (Golf)

#2: Basketball

#3: Defense

#4: Boxing

#5: High Jump

#6: Badminton

#7: Spike (Volleyball)

#8: Two Points

#9: Jump Rope Backwards

Page 14

#1: Quarter (Football)

#2: Archery

#3: Racquet Ball

#4: Gatorade

#5: Gymnastics

#6: Captain

#7: Hockey

#8: Tee Ball

#9: Jumping Jacks

Getting-To-Know-You Adventures

Age Appeal: Fourth Grade and Up   `Also good for teens, adults, and seniors`

Purpose: Interpersonal skills

Equipment: Copies of prepared sheets
for participants

Pencils and/or pens

Group Size: Any size

Setting: Gym or classroom

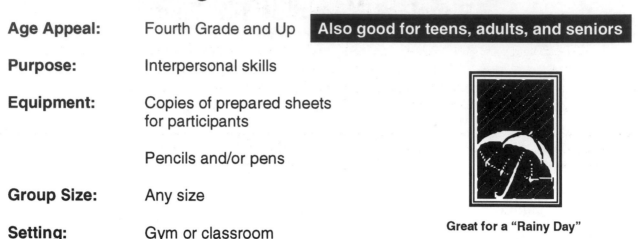

Great for a "Rainy Day"

DESCRIPTION: These "Getting-to-Know-You" activities are great ice breakers to do at the beginning of the year. They are nonthreatening in nature and really do provide some insight into the interests and previous experiences of your students. We have three "Getting-to-Know-You" activities just for you!

- Human Bingo
- Yellow Brick Road Scavenger Hunt
- Where in the World Is...

Please feel free to use the activities as you see fit. Each activity requires that all of the students have their own sheet and a pencil or pen. The object is for players to get autographs of other participants that fit the description requested in each square on the paper. After all of the instructions are given, the students are free to move about the room gathering signatures from students who match the descriptions on the sheet. General rules include:

- A student can only autograph another student's paper once. This allows for greater student interaction.

- When the sheet is completed or playing time is over, participants should return to their seats or a designated place in the gym. The students can share how many squares or questions they have completed on the sheet. The teacher can also review the list of questions.

Teacher Tips:

- Since these are getting-to-know-you activities, finishing quickly should not be emphasized, but rather taking time to converse with others while playing.
- Human Bingo usually takes a few minutes longer to play than the other two activities.

HUMAN BINGO

Directions: In this game, you are challenged to get the autographs of other individuals that fit the description found in each of the squares below. You may get the signature of each person only one time. Try to fill up all of the squares before time is called. Good luck!

First name begins with an "S"	Has brown eyes	Last name begins with an "S"	Wears glasses	Has been to summer camp
Is an "only" child	Was born out of this state	Wears a watch	Likes to play soccer	Has 3 or more brothers or sisters
Eats two or more fruits or vegetables a day	Likes physical education!	**FREE SPACE** (Anyone can sign here)	Can roller-skate	Has long hair
Has been to a professional baseball game	Is left-handed	Likes to swim	Can name 3 states that begin with the letter "N"	Has been to the Grand Canyon
Likes to draw	Has curly hair	Knows what the "Heimlich maneuver" is	Can tie shoes with eyes closed	Has been to the state capitol

Great Activities Publishing Company

YELLOW BRICK ROAD SCAVENGER HUNT

Directions: In this game, you are challenged to follow the Yellow Brick Road and get an autograph of anyone who fits the descriptions listed on the bricks along the way...

START HERE! Has seen the "Wizard of Oz"	Has slept in a tent	Has never had poison ivy	Can spell "Kansas"	Has a small black dog
				Likes to walk or hike
Can outrun a winged monkey!	Can name Dorothy's three companions	Knows someone who lives on a farm	Can ride a bike	Can sing "Somewhere Over the Rainbow"
Has a nice smile				
Likes to dance	Does chores at home	Has seen or helped make a scarecrow	Has courage	**FINISH!** Has seen a real hot air balloon!

Great Activities Publishing Company

WHERE IN THE WORLD IS...

Directions: In this game, you are a special detective and are looking for individuals who fit the following descriptions.

Assignment #1:
Get the fingerprints (signatures) of three people who are your age:

#1:	#2:	#3:

Assignment #2:
Get the fingerprints (signatures) of a person who:

Has been to a foreign country:	Has taken a trip on a train:	Has found a lost ring or a set of keys:

Assignment #3
Get the fingerprints (signatures) of a person who:

Likes chocolate ice cream:	Has black hair	Can name his or her first grade teacher

Last Assignment:
Do the following and get this person's fingerprint (signature):

Shake hands with a person born in September:	Introduce yourself to someone with your same shoe size:	Find someone about your height:

Great Activities Publishing Company

VBI (Visible, But Inconspicuous)

Age Appeal: Fourth Grade and Up   **Also good for teens, adults, and seniors**

Purpose: Interpersonal skills

Equipment: Numerous items as listed on the sheet,
Envelopes,
Pencils and/or pens,
Tape

Group Size: Any size

Setting: Gym or classroom

Great for a "Rainy Day"

DESCRIPTION: This activity is just plain fun! It is an observation game that has been very successful for developing social interaction. The game is especially useful after a winter or spring vacation as it can help to reacquaint the students in a nonthreatening manner. The object is for players to discover the hidden items on the other players and then write down the wearer's name on a line opposite the listed item. A list of suggested items and actual directions for playing are found on the next page. Instructions and one item can be placed in an envelope prior to playing and given to the students before the game begins.

These instructions are placed in an envelope with each item:

> "Take the item enclosed in this envelope and place it somewhere on you that is visible but inconspicuous. Do not let anyone see you hide it and do not show anyone where it is located or what it is. Be sure that at least part of your item is visible. If you need tape, go to the table. After your item is hidden, pick up the V.B.I. (Visible, But Inconspicuous) sheet from your teacher."

Teacher Tips:

- At end of game, recognize those who have the most names on their sheet.
- Also see if any players have items that have never been detected.
- Placing the items in the envelopes requires a bit of preparation, but it's worth the effort! (Perhaps a parent could help you with this!)

Welcome to the "I Spy" V.B.I. Party!

Directions: Beginning now, and until the teacher signals to stop, try to meet as many people as you can and discover the V.B.I. (Visible, But Inconspicuous) item that has been "planted." Each person has been given only one item from the list below, but several people may have the same item. When you spot an item, introduce yourself and then write down the wearer's name in the blank space. Don't tell anyone. Can you find more than 20 items before time runs out?

Man's Tie_____	Pen _____
Toothpick_____	Baseball Card_____
Plastic Bracelet _____	Clothespin _____
Canceled Stamp_____	Marble_____
Golf Pencil_____	Piece Of Candy_____
Balloon_____	Seashell _____
Cotton Ball_____	Thimble_____
Rubber Band_____	Button_____
Penny_____	Safety Pin_____
Paper Clip_____	Thread _____
Magic marker_____	Stocking _____
Nail _____	Key _____
Piece of Yarn _____	Sandwich Bag _____
Earring _____	Rag _____
Adhesive Tape_____	Peanut _____
Plastic Action Figure _____	Flower_____
Toothbrush_____	Playing Card_____

Great Activities Publishing Company

The Blanket Name Game

Age Appeal:	Third Grade and Up `Also good for teens`
Purpose:	Interpersonal skills
Equipment:	A full-sized sheet or blanket per group
Group Size:	10-15 players per group
Setting:	Gym, classroom, or outdoors

DESCRIPTION: This is a fun ice breaker that can be used at various times during the school year, especially as a "back-to-school" activity! It is an enjoyable way for the students to get to know one another. Players are divided into two teams and seated on opposite sides of a blanket held up by two students. The players should sit back away from the blanket, and in position so they cannot be seen by the players on the other side.

To begin, one member from each team moves close to and faces the blanket. On a signal ("1-2-3-GO!"), the two players holding the blanket drop it and each "close" player strives to be first to call out the name of the person facing him/her. Whichever player calls out the correct name first is the winner of the round. The loser must then change teams by joining the group on the other side of the blanket.

The game continues with two more players - one from each side - sitting on each side of the raised blanket. The game is finished when all players are on one side or when time runs out.

Teacher Tips:

- Let the players decide who approaches the blanket. No special order is required. You will find your students will become very creative in how and where they "crouch" behind the blanket. This adds to the fun of the game.

- Remind the students not to position themselves so that they can be seen by the players on the other team. If the game is played outdoors, tell the students that <u>even their shadows</u> showing through the blanket may give the other team clues.

Bumpity, Bump, Bump, Bump!

Age Appeal: Third Grade and Up | **Also good for teens and adults**

Purpose: Interpersonal skills

Equipment: None

Group Size: Divide your class into groups of 6-8 players

Setting: Gym, classroom, or outdoors

DESCRIPTION: All of the players stand in a circle facing inward. One player is IT and stands in the center of the circle. The other players in the circle should know names of people standing on their right and left.

To begin the game, IT goes and stands in front of a player in the circle and points to this player and says either the word "right" or "left" followed by "bumpity, bump, bump, bump." The player pointed to must quickly say the name of the person to his right or left side before IT can say "bumpity, bump, bump, bump."

If the player in the circle does say the correct name in the allotted time, IT moves on to try to catch another player. If the player in the circle is too slow or says the wrong name, he then joins IT in the middle. The game is over when there are more ITS in the center than players in the circle, or until time is up.

Teacher Tips:

- When the "caught" players join IT in the middle, there will be a wider space left in the circle. Players should be instructed to move together quickly and to learn the name of the person on the other side of the vacant space(s) to avoid being caught.

Name Exercises

Age Appeal: Grades K-3

Purpose: Creative thinking and interpersonal skills

Equipment: None

Group Size: 15-30 players

Setting: Gym, classroom, or outdoors

DESCRIPTION: All of the players stand in a circle and one by one introduce themselves by saying their first and last name. Once everyone has said his or her name, the students put an action to each syllable of their first and last names. Here is an example for the name "Richard Brown."

Syllable:	Gesture:
"Rich" ⟶	Jump and spread feet apart
"ard" ⟶	Jump and put feet together
"Brown" ⟶	Quickly lift both hands overhead

Together the group repeats the name and the actions three or four times. The game continues with everyone selecting actions for each syllable of his name. What a fun way to exercise!

I Like People Who ...

Great for a "Rainy Day"

Age Appeal: Fifth Grade and Up   Also good for teens and adults

Purpose: Interpersonal skills

Equipment: One chair for every player. (Poly spots, carpet squares, or other objects can also be used if the game is played in the gym or outside.)

Group Size: 15-30 players per group

Setting: Gym, classroom, or outdoors

DESCRIPTION: This activity is a great getting-to-know-you energizer! While it is somewhat competitive in nature, the game lends itself to even the shyest of players. The players sit in chairs (or stand on poly spots) in circle formation. One person is the leader and stands in the center and completes the statement –"I like people who . . ." If the statement is true about players sitting in the circle, they must change chairs. At the same time, the person in the center tries to get a seat. The player without a seat to sit in becomes the new leader. Here are a few examples:

Statement:	Action:
"I like people who like to talk!"	Everyone who likes to talk finds a new seat.
"I like people who have a dog!"	Everyone who has a dog finds a new seat.
"I like people who wear a watch!"	Everyone wearing a watch finds a new seat.

The game continues as the player without a chair stands in the center and completes a new sentence. Play as long as desired. Of course, there should be only one chair or spot for each player in the circle, no extras.

Partner Interviews

Age Appeal: Fifth Grade and Up   **Also good for teens, adults, and seniors**

Purpose: Oral presentation and interpersonal skills

Equipment: None

Group Size: 10-30

Setting: Anywhere!

DESCRIPTION: This is a low-key and nonthreatening activity to help students feel more comfortable with each other at the beginning of the school year. Each member of the class selects a partner. The partners go off to a quiet spot nearby and interview each other. Discovering interesting and unique facts make the game more fun. After about 5 minutes, the group comes back together and sits in a large circle. Partners should sit together. The players then introduce their partners to the group, sharing the information learned from the interviews.

Teacher Tips:

- As the teacher presides, ask for volunteers at random to take turns. Both partners will introduce each other before moving on to another couple.

- At the conclusion of the game, participants are invited to add interesting facts about group members or themselves. If time permits, questions may be asked and answered.

- This is a great game because everyone has a chance to speak, and it is often easier to share facts about others than about yourself.

- This activity could be a writing assignment incorporating typical questions for gathering information with an interview format.

Name Call Ball

Age Appeal: Third Grade and Up   **Also good for teens and adults**

Purpose: Social skills

Equipment: Several medium-sized foam balls

Group Size: 12-20 players per group works best

Setting: Gym or outdoors

DESCRIPTION: Name Call Ball is a great activity to develop and maintain an atmosphere of openess and group togetherness. The players stand in a circle facing inward. The game starts by giving the ball to the first student. This player says his name to the group. The ball is handed around the circle, with each player in turn telling the group his name. Once everyone has said his name, the ball is tossed at random to players. Before throwing, however, the "thrower" must call out the name and get the attention of the person to whom the ball is being thrown. The "receiver" will say "Thank you, _____ ," calling out the name of the person who threw the ball. As the game progresses, more balls can be added.

Teacher Tips:

- When playing with people who already know each other, precede each name with a descriptive adjective, such as "Happy Jane" or "Busy Jim." Participants will give themselves the descriptive adjective before play begins.

- Emphasize throwing the ball so it can be caught easily. Also be sure that the catcher is ready and expecting it. Balls should be soft enough and large enough to be easily handled.

Sit Down

Age Appeal: Grades K-5

Purpose: Social skills

Equipment: Chairs

Group Size: Any Size

Setting: Gym, classroom, or outdoors

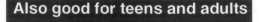

Also good for teens and adults

Great for a "Rainy Day"

DESCRIPTION: This is another great "get acquainted" game. It can be used to help the teacher become more familiar with the students and their personalities. The teacher prepares a list of items in advance that describe students in class. All of the students stand in front of their chairs in a large circle formation. The teacher then begins to read an item from the list in this manner:

- "Sit down if you are wearing red socks!" All of the players wearing red socks sit down. The teacher then continues by reading a second statement.

- "Sit down if you made an A on the last spelling test." Play continues until 5 or 6 such statements have been shared. The leader might then read a generalized statement that would probably describe those left standing—"Sit down if you like chocolate ice cream." To begin the next round, all players again stand and play resumes for several more rounds.

Teacher Tips:

- "Stand Up and Yell" is a variation of this game. Instead of all players standing to begin the game, they stay seated until a statement describes them. When it does, they jump up, put both arms in the air overhead and yell.

- Another variation is to have the players stand when a statement applies to them and remain standing. If another statement applies to them, they sit down. During this game the players are intermittently sitting or standing throughout. This version creates a lot more action!

Spin A Yarn

Age Appeal: Third Grade and Up   **Also good for teens, adults, and seniors**

Purpose: Interpersonal skills, also
memory recall skills

Equipment: One prepared ball of yarn
for each group

Group Size: Small groups of 5-7 players

Setting: Gym, classroom, or outdoors

Great for a "Rainy Day"

DESCRIPTION: This game will help your students get to know one another in a casual and relaxed setting. Divide the class into small groups of 5-7 players. The players sit in a circle with one player holding a ball of yarn and the person on the left holding the end of the yarn. The yarn ball is made up of at least two different colors, tied together in lengths of a yard or less (varied lengths). For example, the ball of yarn could be made from red and blue yarn. Each piece of blue yarn is about a yard long and is tied to a length of red yarn about a yard long. The red and blue yarn pieces are bound into a small ball of yarn with a total length of 15-20 yards.

Play begins as the person holding the end of the yarn begins to wind the yarn back into a ball. As the player winds the yarn into a ball, he or she talks on a certain topic, such as "what I did during the summer," "what I like to do," or "my favorite hobby is." This person talks only as long as one color is being wound. When the color changes, play stops, and the yarn ball is passed to the next player. Now this new player begins to talk and roll up the next length of yarn. Play continues until each player has had a turn or until the entire yarn ball has been rewound.

Teacher Tips:

- Demonstrate this game to the students before playing.

- Try using this game as a way to review for a test or quiz. Each of the students can be asked to tell all they know about the content for a test or quiz. For example, "Name as many states and capitals as you can," "Recite the six times tables," or "List as many Presidents as you can."

- For visually impaired students, you can alternate yarn and string when making the yarn balls. In this way, it is easier to feel the texture of the materials change. It's also a good method to use when playing this game in the dark around a camp fire.

Group Blind Walk

Age Appeal: Fourth Grade and Up

Purpose: Trust-building skills

Equipment: Blindfolds

Group Size: Any Size

Setting: Outdoors

DESCRIPTION: In this activity, the participants are challenged to hold hands and move as a group from one end of a large field to the other. Before play begins, a few minutes are needed for the group members to discuss how they will cross the field. They may line up in any formation, but must stay together by holding hands or linking elbows and have their blindfolds on. Talking is permitted throughout the activity.

A predetermined signal (whistle) should be established so that players know when to stop and listen for directions from the teacher. Extra student helpers can accompany the group to serve as "spotters." These students will help the group stay clear of any trees or other obstacles.

Teacher Tips: Blindfold activities must be conducted in a safe environment and the students must be well-informed. Anytime one of our senses is taken away, we realize just how much we take it for granted. Blindfold activities are no exception, and may be somewhat challenging and uncomfortable for a few of your students.

- Remind the students that completing the task as a group is important. The purpose of the blindfold is to help people remember not to look. If you feel you must, anyone can peek from under the blindfold.

- There are several ways to make a blindfold. One way is to use a basic face mask and seal the eye holes with masking tape. Another way is to fold a bandana into a strip, tie a knot in one end and a rubber band in the other end. Then loop the rubber band around the knot in the back of the head for a comfortable fit!

Partner Blind Walk

Age Appeal: Fourth Grade and Up

Purpose: Trust-building skills

Equipment: Blindfolds

Group Size: Any Size

Setting: Outdoors

DESCRIPTION: This is a partner trust-building activity. Each student selects a partner. One partner is blindfolded, while the other stands behind him. The object of this activity is for the sighted partner to help the blindfolded partner walk to a predetermined goal about 100-150 yards away. The sighted partner gives minimal directions (only speaks when necessary) as the blindfolded partner is guided to the goal. When the blindfolded partner thinks he has reached the goal, he asks "Am I there?" If within three feet of the goal, the partner answers "Yes." If not, more directions are given. When the goal is reached, the partners go back to the starting line, switch roles, and begin again.

Tanks

Age Appeal: Fourth Grade and Up

Purpose: Trust-building skills

Equipment: Blindfolds and soft foam balls and/or gertie balls

Group Size: Any Size

Setting: Indoors or Outdoors

DESCRIPTION: Each student selects a partner. One partner is blindfolded (Tank), the other stands behind the blindfolded partner (Driver). The object of this activity is for the sighted partner to help the blindfolded partner pick up one of the soft foam balls scattered about the playing area and hit another "Tank" below the shoulders.

To begin play, all partners stand on the outside edge of the playing area. The "Tanks" put on their blindfolds. On the leader's signal, they move into the playing area. The "Drivers" verbally direct the "Tanks" to locate one of the many balls in the playing area. When a ball is picked up, the "Drivers" give directions where to throw the ball. If a "Tank" is hit (blown up) by a ball, the "Driver" and "Tank" change places and continue to play. Drivers can also deflect oncoming balls so that they will not hit the "Tank."

Barnyard

Age Appeal: Third Grade and Up   **Also good for teens and adults**

Purpose: Trust-building and social skills

Equipment: Blindfolds (optional)

Group Size: Small (12-20)

Setting: Gym

DESCRIPTION: This is a great activity that can be played with or without blindfolds. If played without blindfolds, the players should close their eyes. One by one, the participants are given the name of an animal (dog, cow, cat, or pig) by the teacher. The students then scatter in the play area and put on a blindfold (or close their eyes).

On a signal from the leader, players yell out the sound made by their particular animal ("bark", "moo," "meow," or "oink.") and move about to find others making the same sound. When such a person is found, the two connect and continue to find all others with the same sound. When the activity is over, the teacher will direct the players to remove their blindfolds.

Teacher Tips:	• This game is a quick, easy, and creative way to form teams. A different animal is designated for as many teams as desired. For example: ducks, sheep, and turkeys could be used if you wanted to divide the class into three different groups. • The teacher whispers the name of the animal to each person so no one else can hear. • Players should keep hands out in front (bumpers up position) and spotters should make sure blindfolded players remain safe.

Blindfold Line Up

Age Appeal: Fifth Grade and Up

Purpose: Trust-building and problem-solving skills

Equipment: Blindfolds

Group Size: Small (12-20 players)

Setting: Gym or playground

DESCRIPTION: Divide the class into groups of 8-12 players. Each group is designated a specific location where it can perform the activities safely and without interference. To begin, all participants are asked to put on a blindfold. Several rounds of this activity can be played with a different task given by the leader:

Round #1:   Line up by birthdate (month and day born).

Round #2:   Line up by height (shortest to tallest).

Round #3:   Line up by number. In this activity, the participants stand in a circle facing inward. Everyone puts on a blindfold. A leader stands in the middle of the circle. Players extend a fist toward the leader. The leader grabs each fist in turn and calls out a number. When a player has received a number, he drops the arm and backs away until all players have a number. Then play begins.

Teacher Tip:	• Spotters and assistants are needed for safety and to guide strayed players back to their group.

Blizzard

Age Appeal: Fifth Grade and Up

Purpose: Trust-building and problem-solving skills

Equipment: Blindfolds and other items to make the obstacle course

Group Size: Small (12-20 players)

Setting: Gym or playground

DESCRIPTION: Each player has a partner. One partner is blindfolded and is led by the other partner through an obstacle course (over, under, between, through). A blizzard has "snow blinded" one player, and a friend must lead him through the blizzard to safety. They must travel through a snow tunnel, under an ice log, over a frozen river, across a snow bridge, etc. Once they reach safety, partners switch roles.

Teacher Tips: • The activity can be played with another theme such as guiding an airplane pilot through a heavy fog.

         • Instead of leading a partner by hand, the blindfolded person is led by:

            1. Verbal cues.

            2. Percussion cues (clapping when going wrong, snapping fingers when going right).

            3. A particular code created by partners.

Obstacle Walk

Age Appeal: Fifth Grade and Up

Purpose: Trust-building skills

Equipment: Blindfolds

Group Size: Small (8-12 players)

Setting: Gym or outdoors in a safe area

DESCRIPTION: The group lines up one behind the other with hands on shoulders or waist of person in front. Blindfolds are on. A leader at the head of the line leads the group over, under, around, and up and down an obstacle type course. The leader can see (of course) but cannot speak. The group can talk, but cannot see. Players must stay in contact with each other. A spotter is helpful to follow with the group for safety purposes. The leader should plan ahead and know the course to be traveled.

Teacher Tips:	•	Project Adventure calls this activity a "Sherpa Walk" and uses the fantasy story about an annual trip the natives of a far away country must take. This story is told before the activity begins. It seems that the natives were born without sight, so they hired a guide to lead them on their journey. The only guides they could find could not speak, but together they could travel successfully.
	•	The game usually takes about 15-20 minutes.

Sculpture Charades

Age Appeal: Fourth Grade and Up

Purpose: Social interaction and creative thinking skills

Equipment: None

Group Size: Any size

Setting: Gym, classroom, or outdoors

DESCRIPTION: Divide the class into groups of 5-8 students. The groups sit in scattered formation around the playing area. One member from each group comes up to the leader who whispers a word to him. This player returns to his group and "molds" the player on his right into a shape that depicts the word.

Suggested Words: Statue of Liberty, horse, baby, Santa Claus, tree, fried egg, etc.

The rest of the group tries to guess the word. When the word is guessed, another member of the group comes up to the leader, gets a new word, and hurries back to continue. Play continues for 6-8 rounds. Game is over when most groups have guessed all of the words.

Shape the Rope

Age Appeal: Third Grade and Up

Purpose: Group cooperation and problem-solving skills

Equipment: Blindfolds, a large rope tied in a circle

Group Size: Small groups of 8-15 players

Setting: Gym or outdoors

DESCRIPTION: Divide the class into groups of 8-15 students. Each participant is given a blindfold and the group is given a large rope. Participants stand facing inward and hold onto a circle of rope with both hands. Players then close their eyes or put on blindfolds. A leader calls out a shape (square, triangle, polygon, rectangle, etc.).

Without letting go of the rope, the group works together to make that shape. When players agree that they are finished, they open their eyes or remove their blindfolds to view their results. Play continues as the leader calls out another shape.

Attitude

By Charles Swindoll

The longer I live, the more I realize the impact of attitude on life. Attitude, to me, is more important than facts. It is more important than the past, than education, than money, than circumstances, than failures, than successes, than what other people think or say or do.

It is more important than appearance, giftedness or skill. It will make or break a company... a church... a home. The remarkable thing is that we have a choice every day regarding the attitude we will embrace for that day. We cannot change our past... we cannot change the fact that people will act in a certain way. We cannot change the inevitable.

The only thing we can do is play on the one string we have and that is our attitude. I am convinced that life is 10% what happens to me and 90% how I react to it. And so it is with you. We are in charge of our attitudes.

2 Cooperative Games:
"Bright Sparklers for All!"

Chapter Overview: Now that you and your students have had loads of fun getting to know each other, let's take a look at a few group games that can be played indoors or outside. The activities in this chapter will give you scores of teacher-tested games that can be played with limited or no equipment.

Discipline Tip #1: Minor Student Distractions

Spaced throughout this book are eight different sets of teaching tips for handling student behaviors. Here are a few ideas that will help you "nip it in the bud."

Handling Minor Distractions: If the misconduct is of short duration, is not dangerous and does not merit disrupting the class or activity, usually it can be corrected by one or more of the following strategies:

- Make Eye Contact! Making eye contact with the person causing a disturbance.
- Stop Speaking! Refraining from speaking until the disturbance is over (ie. people talking when they should be listening).
- Move In! Moving closer and standing near the person causing a disturbance.
- Give Them a Hand! Placing a hand on the offender.
- Take a Stand! Standing between offenders.

No Mixed Signals: It is wise for a leader/teacher to establish a signal for listening. This signal or cue can be used to remind the students that their full attention is needed and they should refrain from talking. Cues may include:

- All Hands on Deck! Hand held high in the air overhead. (When the hand goes up, the mouth closes tight and all eyes are on the leader.)
- Listen Up! Sounding a whistle, clicker, or a soft drum beat.
- Music Magic! Using music to start an activity or to signal when it is over.
- Lights Out! Using the lights, switched off then on.
- Quiet Encounters! Counting to 10.

When teaching children to respond to the established signal, practice by playing a game with them which emphasizes a quick response. For example, if you decide that "counting to ten" is your signal, then play a game that challenges them to perform a certain task before you count to ten. Example: "Let's play the Countdown Game! I'll give you ten seconds to follow my commands. Who can run to the far gym wall, touch it and quietly sit back down in your original spot? Go! 10, 9, 8, ...etc. That was great! Now, who can skip around the gym without bumping into another student? Go! 10, ... 9, ... 8, ... (slowly counting).. etc. Wonderful! Now, who can quickly shake hands with three different people, sit down, and be quiet? Go! 10, 9, 8, ... etc. Wow! What a great job!"

Clap Rhythm

Age Appeal: Grades K-5   **Also good for teens, adults, and seniors**

Purpose: Listening, sequencing, and short-term memory skills

Equipment: Lively music!

Group Size: Any Size

Setting: Gym, classroom, or outdoors

Great for a "Rainy Day"

DESCRIPTION: Students may sit or stand. On your command, the students follow a series of hand and arm actions set to music. Prior to starting, the group follows the teacher through a practice sequence of about 15 actions. Practice a couple of times before actually beginning with music. It is not necessary for the students to memorize the sequence, since they can follow the teacher throughout the activity. It is important that the teacher learns the routine!

Sample Clap Rhythm:

1. Clap own knees twice.
2. Clap own hands twice.
3. "Miss" clap one way. (2 counts)
4. "Miss" clap the other way. (2 counts)
5. Hit fists together twice.
6. Hit fists together the other way twice.
7. Touch elbow with right hand and with left arm bent, shake pointer finger twice.
8. Repeat 7 with the other hand and arm twice.
9. Make swimming motions with left hand and arm, then with right hand and arm. Repeat again with left, then right. (4 counts for each hand-arm)
10. Make breast stroke swimming motion with both hands and arms twice.
11. Move left hand and arm in lasso fashion over head.
12. Repeat 11 with right hand and arm.
13. Move left hand and arm in hitchhiking fashion to left.
14. Repeat 13 with right hand and arm.
15. Reach up in the air and catch an imaginary bug (or magic dust), put it in your hands, roll it around, look someone in the eye and blow it on them.
16. Begin clap rhythm again and continue until end of music.

Cooperative Counting

Age Appeal:	Third Grade and Up

Also good for teens, adults, and seniors

Purpose:	Cooperation and interpersonal skills
Equipment:	None
Group Size:	Any Size
Setting:	Gym, classroom, or outdoors

Great for a "Rainy Day"

DESCRIPTION: This is a very challenging and funny game that always gets the students laughing! It's harder than it sounds. The students stand in a large circle. The object of the game is to see if the group is able to count to 20 without anyone speaking at the same time. Anyone can begin, but if two people say a number simultaneously, then play begins again at number 1. Players should not gesture in any way before speaking.

Teacher Tips:

- Remind the players that this game must be completed with no preplanning, organizing, or calling out the numbers in a set order.

- If the group has difficulty, the goal can be changed from counting to 20 to a lower number, such as 12.

Sit Down Square Dancing

Great for a "Rainy Day"

Age Appeal: Grades K-5   **Also good for teens, adults, and seniors**

Purpose: Listening and group cooperation skills

Equipment: Lively instrumental square dance music! (**Note:** There are several fun tunes on the cassette "Awesome Heart-Healthy Dances" produced by Great Activities Publishing Company. Call 1 (800) 927-0682 to order this tape.)

Group Size: Any Size

Setting: Gym, classroom, or outdoors

DESCRIPTION: This is an all-time favorite! It is a fun way to incorporate listening skills into a fun lead-up activity for square dancing. Sit Down Square Dance is just what the title implies, moving body parts in any way possible while in a seated position. For groups unable to dance with their feet (disabled, elderly) or in a situation where there is a lack of space or even in a group of reluctant participants, this type of dancing is a "winner." Square dance type music is played in the background and a "caller" directs the group in a variety of movements. Some ideas for calls are:

1. "Circle right and left"- hold hands with person on either side and keep time with the music as you lean to the side and bounce with the beat.

2. "Into the center with a hoot and a shout"- lean down, bounce and yell; lean out or sit back up as you bounce to the beat of the music.

3. "Clap your hands," your knees; the floor; your head or other body parts.

4. "Clap your partner's knees," hands, back, head, etc.

5. "Make your shoulders go up and down."

6. "Wiggle your nose," or ears.

7. "Stomp the floor with your feet," or hands.

8. "Bow to your neighbor."

The Sharing Circle

Age Appeal:	Grades K-6	**Also good for teens, adults, and seniors**
Purpose:	Social interaction and reflective thinking skills	
Equipment:	None	
Group Size:	Any Size	
Setting:	Gym, classroom, or outdoors	

DESCRIPTION: This is a great way to bring closure to a class, course, or meeting. It allows the students to give important personal feedback to the group as a whole. This activity originated with the Eskimos of Canada. The participants stand facing inward in a circle with arms around the backs of people on each side. The object of the activity is to give anyone who wishes an opportunity to speak. A leader sets the stage by giving directions and announcing the subject.

The subject could be the participants' opinions about a course or class. It could be a form of review after a lesson. To play, a statement is made at random by a member of the group. The group follows each statement with a few steps in one direction, moving sidewards. After a second statement, made by another member of the group, everyone shuffles a few steps in the opposite direction. This procedure continues until everyone who wishes has had an opportunity to speak. The leader makes a final closing statement and the activity ends.

Teacher Tip: If this activity is used outdoors, this final comment can be made by the teacher or leader: "Everyone let go of the person next to you, and take two steps back. Notice the circle that has been etched on the ground where we shuffled. We can think of this as our circle of friendship."

Circle Lap Sit

Age Appeal: Third Grade and Up   Also good for teens and adults

Purpose: Group cooperation and teamwork skills

Equipment: None

Group Size: For ten or more players

Setting: Gym, classroom, or outdoors

DESCRIPTION: The players stand in a tight circle with their hands on the waist of the person in front. The object of this activity is for each student to sit in unison on the knees of the person behind while at the same time guiding the person in front to a seated position onto their knees.

The teacher or leader explains what is to happen and gives the signal for sitting ("1-2-3-sit"). If everyone follows the directions and sits at the same time, a very stable seating is created. Often members of the group do not get a firm seating and fall over. When this happens, the activity begins again. Once success has been accomplished, the leader instructs the participants to remove their hands from the waist of the person in front and enjoy the sitting position for a moment or two. The leader then signals for all to stand again ("1-2-3-stand").

Teacher Tips: If the participants keep falling as they try to sit, instruct them to make a smaller circle by taking a sidewards step toward the center of circle. Remind them that they are responsible for "guiding" the person in front to sit on their knees.

Participants lacking trust will often squat and try to hold up their own weight. To be successful, all must truly sit on the knees of the player behind them. Unequal weight should not be a factor except in extreme weight differences between players.

Variations:

- Once participants are seated, ask them to try to walk forward in this position. The participants will need to use small steps and walk in unison. Example: "Right foot, left foot, right foot, left foot, etc."

- Challenge the group to do the circle lap sit while facing the opposite direction. The participants turn around so that the circle is now facing the other direction before sitting.

Simon Says Twister

Age Appeal: Grades K-3

Purpose: Listening skills and following directions

Equipment: None

Group Size: Any size

Setting: Gym, classroom, or outdoors

DESCRIPTION: To play, the teacher or leader makes a statement. If this statement is true about any of the participants, those students perform an action that is also given by the leader. Here are a few examples:

- Simon says, "If you went to bed on time last night, touch someone's back."

- Simon says, "If you like to play basketball, touch someone's foot."

- Simon says, "If you have a dog as a pet, touch someone's right knee."

- Simon says, "If you have an older brother or a sister, touch someone's left elbow."

The game continues as the leader makes additional statements and directions for other actions. This activity can be played successfully for approximately 10 minutes with young children.

Teacher Tips:	• You may wish to prepare a set of written statements beforehand. This method will allow you to observe the children's responses more easily.
	• This activity can be constructed so that the teacher or leader can gain useful insights about the children. It is fun to have offbeat statements interwoven with information gathering ones.

Busy Bee

Age Appeal: Grades K-3

Purpose: Listening, body part identification, and laterality skills (knowing the difference between "left" and "right")

Equipment: None

Group Size: Any size

Setting: Gym, classroom, or outdoors

DESCRIPTION: Here is another "listen and do" game. Like the game of "Simon Says Twister," this game is a fun and cooperative activity! Players stand back-to-back with a partner. To begin, the leader calls out two body parts and players move quickly to join these two parts. For example:

Command:	Action:
"Elbow to elbow"	Players touch one elbow to their partner's elbow.
"Hand to knee"	Players touch one hand to their partner's knee.
"Left hand to right foot"	Players touch their left hand to their partner's right foot.

After several calls, the leader says "Busy Bee." At this cue, the players change partners by making a buzzing sound and continue "buzzing" until they are standing back-to-back with a new player. The players should be directed not to return to any partner they have had previously.

Play then continues with the leader calling out another set of commands. Play the game long enough so that the children have numerous opportunities to be a "busy bee" and interact with new partners.

Teacher Tips: If there is one player extra, the leader can direct him to:

- Continue buzzing around the play area weaving in and out among the couples until the next call of "Busy Bee."

- Team up as a group of three and complete the task in the best way possible. It really does not matter if there is an extra player; it adds another dimension to the game.

Come Along!

Age Appeal: Grades K-3   **Also good for teens and adults**

Purpose: Social interaction, basic timing, and moving
to the beat of music

Equipment: Lively music

Group Size: Any size

Setting: Gym or outdoors

DESCRIPTION: Using an existing large circle on the gym floor or outside, the players stand on the circle. All of the players walk in a single file around the circle as the music plays. One player is selected to be "IT." This player walks inside the circle in the <u>opposite direction</u> and takes the hand of another player in the circle.

This new player, in turn, chooses and takes the hand of another person from the original circle. One by one, players are taken from the original circle until the entire group is walking to the beat of the music as they hold hands. When the music stops, all of the players quickly move back to find a place on the original circle. The game continues with a new player selected to be "IT."

Elbow Tag

Age Appeal: Third Grade and Up   **Also good for teens and adults**

Purpose: Social interaction and group cooperation skills

Equipment: None

Group Size: A medium sized group of 16 to 30 players

Setting: Gym or outdoors

DESCRIPTION: This is a fun and exciting game that can be played indoors or outside. Players select partners and stand in a large circle. The partners hook elbows and leave enough space for a person to stand on either side of each couple. One player is selected to be the "Chaser" and another player is the "Runner." On the teacher's signal, play begins as the Chaser tries to tag the Runner. Players are not allowed to cut through the circle, but must go around the outside.

The only way the Runner is "safe" is when he hooks up with a player standing in the circle. Once the Runner hooks up with a player in the circle, immediately the partner of that person becomes the new "Runner." Now the Chaser has to try to tag this player. The new Runner quickly moves to either run away from the Chaser or hook up with another couple. If the Chaser get tired, he can hook up with a player. Immediately, that partner becomes the new "Chaser." As the players become better at switching places, the game becomes more fast-paced and exciting!

Fish Gobbler

Age Appeal: Grades K-5

Purpose: Cardiovascular fitness, group cooperation, and listening skills

Equipment: None

Group Size: Any size

Setting: Gym or outdoors

DESCRIPTION: This is a challenging warm-up activity that is a fun cardiovascular fitness game. This is a fantasy-story game designed to get children moving and quickly following directions. Players are scattered about the playing area. Before play begins, participants are familiarized with a vocabulary of movement as follows:

When the Teacher Says:	The Children Will:
"Ship"	Run in direction the teacher is pointing.
"Shore"	Change direction to run in the opposite way.
"Fish Gobbler"	Quickly lie on floor touching another player.

One player is designated as the "Fish Gobbler." When "Fish Gobbler" is called out by the teacher, the Fish Gobbler tries to tag all the children that are not down and connected to another person. Tagged players are "caught" by the Fish Gobbler.

When no more players can be tagged, the Fish Gobbler calls out "Rescue" and all children jump up, holding hands with one or more partners and yell "Yea!" At this point, the game begins again.

Other commands can be added, such as:

When the Teacher Says:	The Children Will:
"Sardines"	Safely get together in a large "group hug."
"Fisherman All"	Sit or hold a person on a knee.
"Fish Net"	Strike a pose of their own choosing.
"Waterspout"	Run in a large clockwise circle

Here, There, and Everywhere

Age Appeal: Grades K-4

Purpose: Cardiovascular fitness, group cooperation, and listening skills

Equipment: None

Group Size: Any size

Setting: Gym or outdoors

DESCRIPTION: This is an easy-to-understand cardiovascular fitness game that is great fun! Have all of the children scatter about the play area, but close enough to hear the teacher speak. The object is for them to follow directions and quickly respond. If the teacher says:

Command:	Action:
"Here"	The children run toward the teacher.
"There"	The children see where the teacher is pointing, and run in that direction.
"Everywhere"	The children run in any direction.

Variations: • You can turn this activity into a fun basketball drill that can be used with fourth through sixth graders by giving all of the students a playground ball or a basketball. The students follow the same commands while dribbling the ball.

I See

Age Appeal: Grades K-3

Purpose: Creative movement skills

Equipment: None

Group Size: Any size

Setting: Gym or outdoors

DESCRIPTION: This is a fun and easy-to-understand game that will help the students develop listening skills as well as creative movement skills. This game involves the children by having them respond to the directions given by the teacher to travel or perform a variety of movements. To begin the game, the teacher says, "I see---" and the children respond, "What do you see?" The teacher then proposes a task for the children to perform immediately. Movement continues until the children again hear the teacher say, "I see---." At this point, they stop and listen for the next assignment. A few examples are:

Teacher:	Children:
"I see" "I see trains moving on a track."	"What do you see?" Students move like trains about the play area.
"I see" "I see an otter swimming on his back."	"What do you see?" Students pretend to swim.
"I see" "I see kids jumping rope."	"What do you see?" Students pretend to jump rope.
"I see" "I see birds flying in the air"	"What do you see?" Students pretend to fly about the play area.
"I see" "I see statues standing still."	"What do you see?" Students stand like statues.
"I see" "I see people hiking up a hill."	"What do you see?" Students pretend to hike up a steep hill.

Sticky Popcorn

Age Appeal: Grades K-4

Purpose: Creative movement skills

Equipment: None

Group Size: Any size

Setting: Gym or outdoors

DESCRIPTION: This is a cooperative group activity that is a fun way to warm-up! Children are instructed to make low, easy jumps as they follow instructions of the teacher. The teacher asks the students to pretend they are popcorn popping. First they jump alone. Then the teacher adds some "butter." This causes the popcorn to join with partners, so the children find a partner and begin jumping in unison by leaning against each other or holding hands.

More butter is added. Now the partners join with another group, all jumping in rhythm together and all connected. Now "syrup" is added. The groups of four join to form groups of eight, then sixteen, and soon the entire class is jumping together! To end the activity, children are instructed to stay where they are "stuck" and slowly melt to the ground.

Teacher Tips:
- This activity is very tiring, so direct the students to get into bigger groups fairly quickly. The entire activity should take less than a minute or two.

- At any point during the activity, children can "melt a little bit" which means they quit jumping and pretend to "wilt" for a few seconds.

Language Arts Game

Age Appeal: Grades 3-5

Purpose: Language arts skills: verbs, adverbs, and prepositions

Equipment: Music and flash cards (Examples are found on the following pages)

Group Size: Any size

Setting: Gym or outdoors

DESCRIPTION: This is a fun language arts curriculum integration game. The students read and then react to a series of flash cards.

Verb Flash Cards:	These are action words. They include words such as: run, jump, hop, bend, dance, twist, crawl, skip, march, slide, gallop, and jog.

Adverb Flash Cards:	These describe the action words and usually end with "ly." They include words such as: slowly, softly, gladly, joyfully, happily, madly, sadly, loudly, swiftly, frightfully, and timidly.

Preposition Flash Cards:	These describe where the actions take place. Words such as: behind, outside, inside, with, under, below, against, near, above, around, down, beside, across, between, up, and over.

The teacher says to the class, "What is your favorite part of speech?" When someone mentions verbs, the teacher says, "I like verbs too. Guess why? Right, they are action words. I am going to play some music and hold up a verb card. I want you to read and then do the action." The teacher then holds up one word at a time, several seconds for each, until all verbs have been acted out.

Next, the teacher holds up a card with the word "Adverb" on it and says, "If verbs tell us what to do, what do you think adverbs do?" When someone answers correctly, the teacher says, "Yes, adverbs tell us how to do the action. Let's read them out loud so that we sound like them." The children then respond to each card as it is held up for them to see. Afterwards, the teacher says, "What did you notice that each word had in common?" The response is usually correct---(they all end in "ly.")

A third part of speech---prepositions---is introduced (or reviewed). The teacher might say: "If verbs tell us what to do and adverbs tell us how to do it, what do you think prepositions do?" After a chance for response, the teacher says, "You are right, prepositions tell us where. I have a set of prepositions such as ---------." After being sure that the children understand and can read the words, the teacher moves on. There is no group action at this point.

The Challenge: Now the children are ready for the challenging part of this activity. Two people help the teacher, and they line up in front of the class, each holding a set of the cards. They stand so the children read a verb, followed by an adverb, and then a preposition. Here is an example: "run" - "slowly" - "behind."

The class is divided into groups of 3-4 children. The object is for them, using each other and working as a group, to respond to the words. They do not all do the same thing (a usual response) but must assume different roles to accurately solve the problem.

Example: with "run" - "slowly" - "behind" they cannot all just run slowly. One person must be first while the other two run slowly behind this player. The activity continues as the cards are changed (each person holding up a new flash card) until all of the cards have been used or the music ends.

Note: A sample set of flash cards is found on the following pages. Please feel free to add additional words to suit your situation.

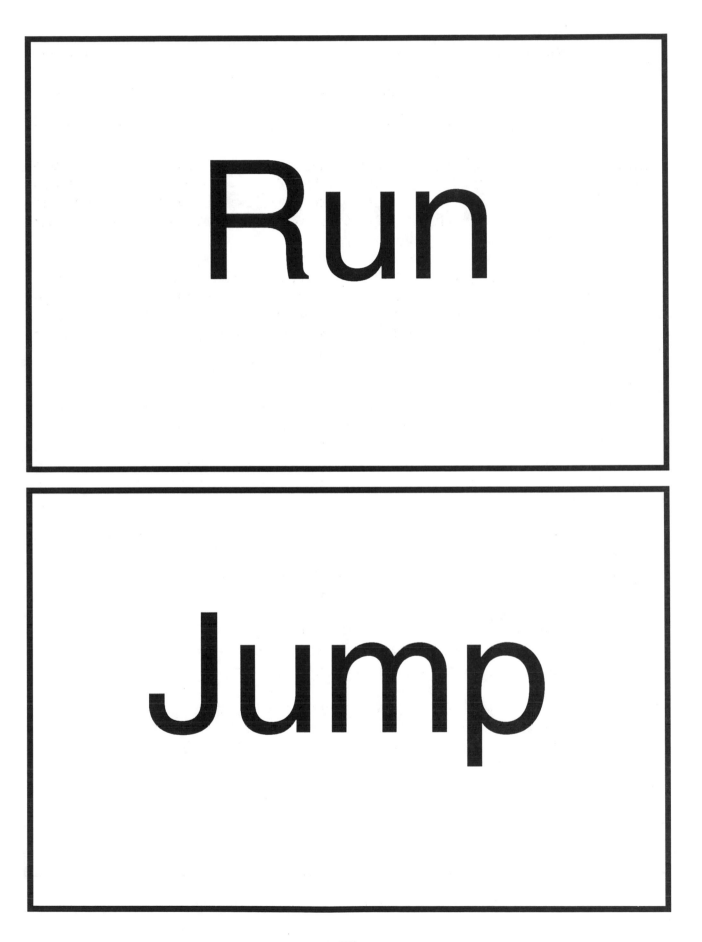

Run

Jump

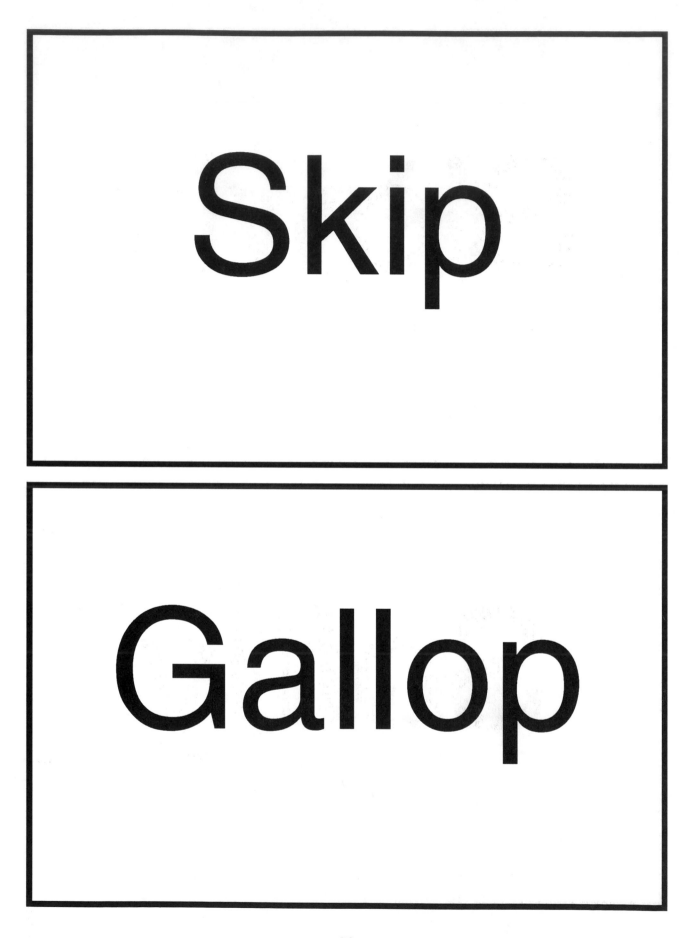

Skip

Gallop

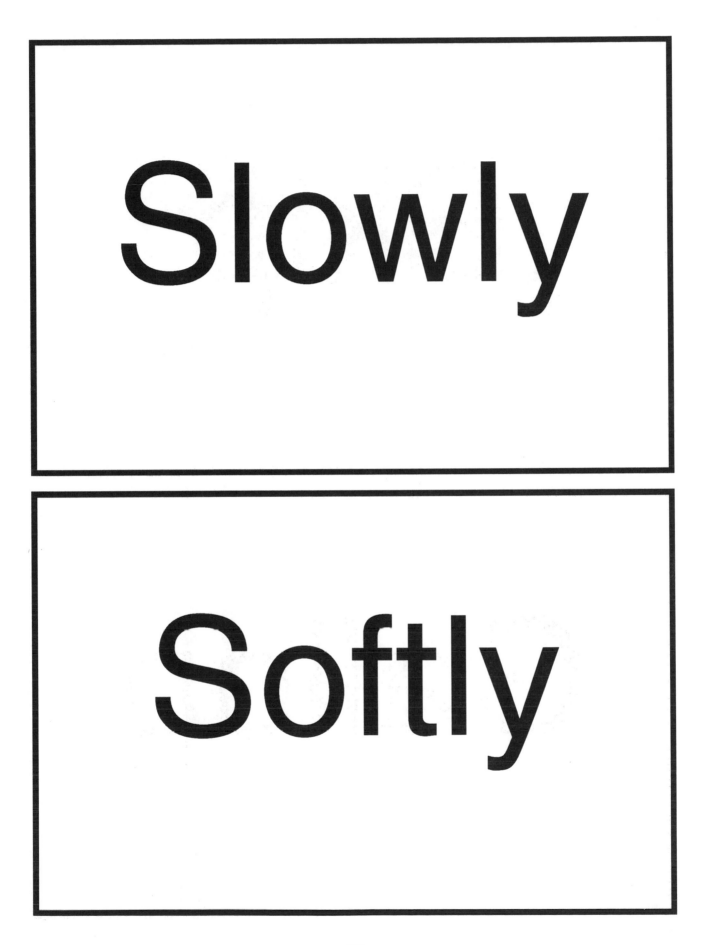

Slowly

Softly

57

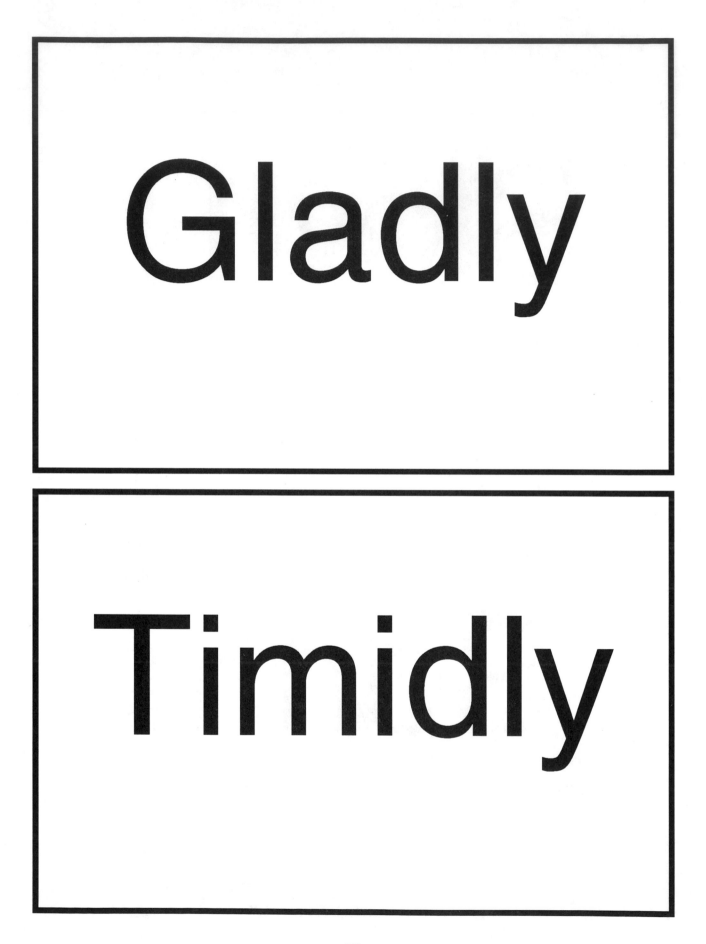

Gladly

Timidly

58

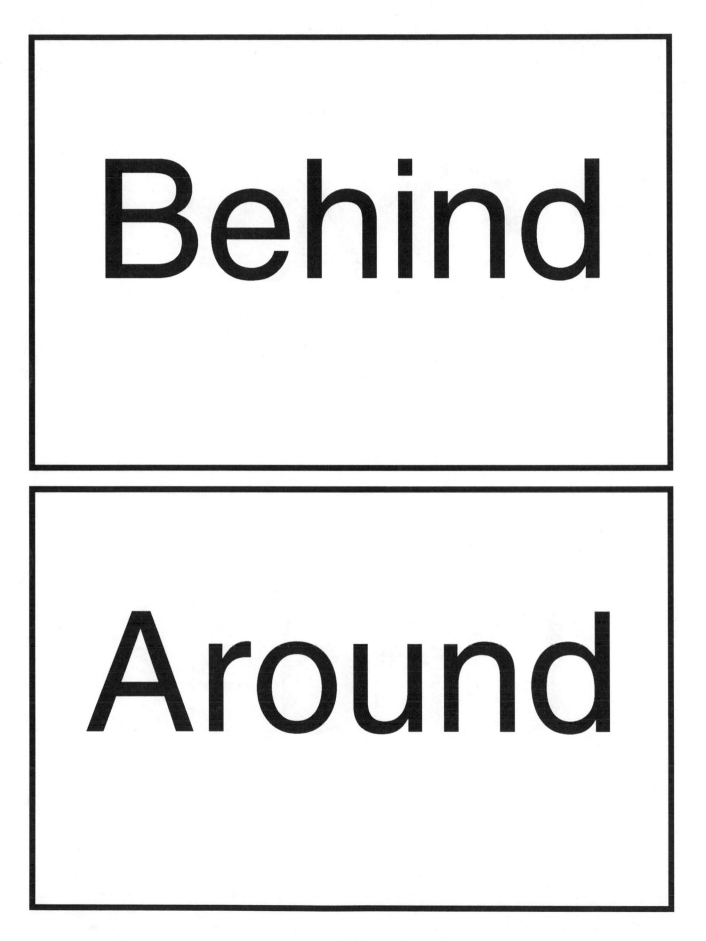

Behind

Around

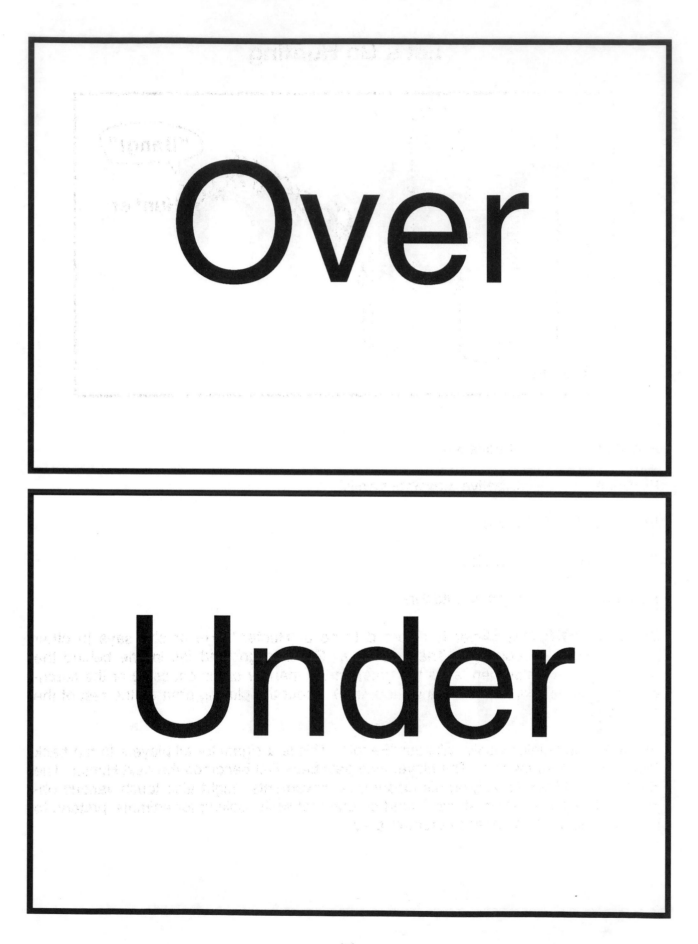

Let's Go Hunting

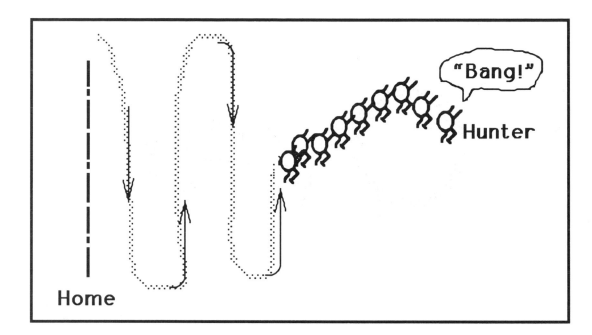

Age Appeal: Grades K-4

Purpose: Creative movement skills

Equipment: None

Group Size: Any size

Setting: Gym or outdoors

DESCRIPTION: One player is selected to be a "Hunter." He or she says to other players, "Let's go hunting." They respond, "Ok, let's go" and fall in line behind the "Hunter." The Hunter then leads the group in the manner of his choosing or the teacher's suggestion (skip, sneak, crawl, hop, etc.) about the playing area as the rest of the class follow.

Suddenly the Hunter loudly calls out "Bang!" This is a signal for all players to run back "home" or to a safety line. The player who gets back first becomes the next Hunter. The Hunter, in addition to varying his locomotive movements, might also touch various objects and perform certain stunts (stand on one foot while looking for animals, pretend to climb a tree, etc.) to enhance creative play.

Samurai Warrior

Age Appeal: Third Grade and Up   **Also good for teens and adults**

Purpose: Agility skills

Equipment: Soft, styrofoam sword or other similar item

Group Size: 10-20

Setting: Gym or outdoors

DESCRIPTION: The teacher or leader is the "Samurai Warrior" and stands with a styrofoam sword in the center of a circle of players. After a series of "formal bows" by the Samurai Warrior to all participants, the game begins. The Warrior swings the sword in either a high arc or a low arc in the direction of people standing in the circle.

If the sword is swung high, participants in the path of the arc must immediately duck. If the sword is swung low, players must immediately jump. Players who jump when they should have ducked, duck when they should have jumped, or do not move at all, are "out" and stand outside the circle. The last player left becomes the new Warrior. A round lasts 2-3 minutes, so players who are out will soon return to the game.

Teaching Tips: • Sound effects (short yells) made by the Warrior while swinging the sword are effective.

• Players should monitor themselves as to jumping and ducking correctly, and remove themselves from the game when they "goof."

Smoug's Jewels

Age Appeal: Third Grade and Up   **Also good for teens and adults**

Purpose: Agility skills

Equipment: Handkerchief or other similar item

Group Size: Small to medium (10-20)

Setting: Gym or outdoors

DESCRIPTION: This game involves the tale from <u>The Hobbit</u> (Tolkein) in which a dragon, Smoug, tries to protect his jewels--thus the name of the game. To play, one person (Smoug) stands over an object such as a handkerchief and tries to keep all other players (who are circled around) from snatching it away.

If Smoug can reach out and tag players, they are frozen for the remainder of the game (usually about one minute). If players can successfully grab the "jewels" (handkerchief), the game begins with the "winner" as the new dragon.

Teaching Tip: A large sponge or a foam ball can be held by Smoug to tag the players.

Squirrels in the Trees

Age Appeal: Grades K-4

Purpose: Cardiovascular fitness

Equipment: None

Group Size: Any size

Setting: Gym or outdoors

DESCRIPTION: Players are divided into groups of 3 and each player is given a number --1, 2, or 3. Players 1 and 2 face each other and hold hands to make a "tree". Player 3 is the "squirrel" and stands "in the tree."

When the leader/teacher calls out, "Squirrels Run!" the squirrels must leave their "tree" and find another tree. "Trees" should be as widely spaced about the playing area as possible. After squirrels are safely settled in a new "tree" the leader again calls "Squirrels Run!" and play continues as before.

The object of the game is to find an "empty tree" that has not been visited. After about 5 calls, the squirrels should change places with number twos and give them a chance to be squirrels. Then after about 5 more calls, the number ones should have a turn as "squirrels."

Teacher Tip: If the playing group is very large, more than 2 players can form the tree, and if the group is very small, circles can be drawn on the floor to designate the trees and all the players can be squirrels.

Help a Friend

Age Appeal: Grades K-3

Purpose: Locomotor and balance skills

Equipment: Bean bags and lively music

Group Size: Any size

Setting: Gym or outdoors

DESCRIPTION: Each player balances a bean bag on a designated body part and moves to the music (walk, skip, slide, etc.) as directed by the teacher. If the bean bag falls off, the player is frozen until an "active" player replaces the bean bag on a body part. If the player helping drops the bean bag in the process of helping, both are frozen until another player unfreezes them.

At the end of the game, ask how many players helped, and make this an important element of the game.

Group Juggling

Age Appeal: Third Grade and Up   Also good for teens and adults

Purpose: Group cooperation, catching and throwing skills

Equipment: Numerous balls

Group Size: Any size

Setting: Gym or outdoors

DESCRIPTION: Divide the class into groups of 8-12 players. Each group stands in a circle facing inward. Before play begins, a pattern of throwing and catching must be established. This is done by the following method:

- One player in each group is designated as the Leader. Each leader has a ball.

- All of the other participants in the circle raise an arm (this signifies that they are available to have a ball thrown to them.)

- The leader begins by throwing a ball to a participant across the circle. That player lowers his or her arm, catches the ball, and in turn throws it to another player across the circle.

- This throwing-catching procedure continues until all participants have received and then thrown the ball.

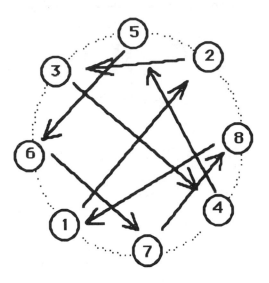

- The leader will be the last person in the circle to receive the ball. Players always throw to the same person and receive from the same person.

- The ball should not be thrown right or left, but across the circle. Once the pattern has been established, the group should practice at least one time before play begins.

Teacher Tips:

- Players should throw so that the ball can be caught--eye contact with receiver should be made before throwing, and the throwing distance must be considered.

- If a poor throw is made or balls collide in midair during play, the ball should be retrieved by a nearby player and put back into play at that point (not returned to player who threw the error.)

- Balls must be large enough and soft enough to be easily caught. Balls should be heavy enough to travel across the circle successfully. Coated foam balls work well. Small balls, like tennis balls, do not work well in this activity.

Play begins when the background music is started and continues for the duration of a song. The leader begins with one ball, but continually adds more balls. The object is to see how successful a group can be in getting as many balls as possible moving at one time. A well-skilled group can get about three-fourths as many balls "going" as there are participants. For example, if there are eight players in a group, they should be able to have six balls moving at the same time without making a mistake.

They Follow Me

Author Unknown

A careful teacher I ought to be,
 Because many children will follow me.
I know I dare not go astray,
 For fear they'll go the selfsame way.

I cannot once escape their eyes,
 Whatever they see me do, they'll try.
Like me they say they're going to be,
 All those kids that follow me.

They think that I am good and fine,
 Believe in every word of mine.
What's base in me they probably see,
 Each one of those that follow me.

I must remember as I go,
 Through summer's sun and winter's snow.
I'm building for the years to see,
 In all those folks who follow me.

3 Moving to Music:
"A Countdown to Fun!"

Chapter Overview: Here's a wonderful selection of fun activities that are good to use with music. Children of all ages seem to enjoy activities more that are associated with lively and upbeat music. You and your students will just love them!

Discipline Tip #2: Step By Step

When Giving Directions: Youngsters always seem to listen better under the following circumstances:

- <u>Get Close Up</u>! Students seem to listen better when the teacher is close to them.
- <u>Off Their Feet</u>! Have the students seated on the floor or in chairs.
- <u>Quiet Please</u>! Limit distractions so your students can easily hear, understand and see.
- <u>It's Only Normal</u>! The leader should speak in a normal voice level (do not yell or scream).
- <u>Are We There Yet</u>? Students tend not to listen when a teacher rambles or repeats a lot. Use concise, well-thought-out directions.
- <u>Don't Pass Out</u>! Delay handing out equipment until directions are explained, demonstrations have been given, and it is time to begin.

A Sequence For Dealing With Misconduct: First analyze and be sure misconduct has not been caused by misunderstanding, or reasons that could be prevented by you.

- <u>Step 1</u> - At the first sign of student misbehavior, speak generally to the group. Remind them of the rules, regulations, standards and guidelines.
- <u>Step 2</u> - Speak directly to the person(s) involved. Have eye contact and if appropriate, tactile contact (place your hand on a shoulder or back). Use their name(s) and tell them exactly what they have done.
- <u>Step 3</u> - Remove the offender from the activity for a short period of time (two or three minutes). This is often called "Time Out." Ask the child to sit in a specific spot away from the game area, to think about what happened and what should have happened, and to stay there until you return. Before returning to the activity, ask the child to tell you how he should act.
- <u>Step 4</u> - Remove the students from the activity for a longer period of time. This action should be accompanied with an individual conference with the student.
- <u>Step 5</u> - Send a letter or make a phone call to the parents/guardians. If a letter is sent, have the parents sign it, respond if appropriate, and return it to you. Make this letter personal, positive and very explicit. <u>Do not send home a form letter!</u> Sending a form letter home gives the parents an impression that many of your students need disciplining. <u>And always follow up</u>! As soon as possible (several days or a week later), contact the parents/guardians again with a positive word of encouragement. Find something good to say and take the time to say it.

Matching Plates

Age Appeal: Grades K-3

Purpose: Basic movement skills, as well as color, shape, and number recognition

Equipment: Homemade paper plates and lively music

Group Size: Any size

Setting: Gym or outdoors

DESCRIPTION: All of the players are given a paper plate. Each plate is different, having a specific shape (square, triangle, circle, or rectangle), color (red, blue, yellow, green), and number (#1-10) on it. The music plays and the students move around the play area. Directions are given by the leader that requests the children to find one or more players that have a likeness (or difference) in one of the items. When the music stops, the players quickly complete the task. Here is an example:

Blue Triangle

Blue Square

Teacher:

"Find a player who has the same shape as yours."

"Find a player who has the same color as yours."

"Find a player who has the same number as yours."

"Find a player(s) so that your numbers add up to equal 12."

"In groups of four or more, arrange your numbers so that the smallest number is first and the largest number is last."

"Get in groups with the same shape and color."

"Get in groups with just the same shape."

More Examples: A plate with a blue triangle and #6 and another plate with a blue square and #4 would match if the leader asks for children to get together with all who have the same color. They would not match if the leader asks for the same shape or number. They would match if the leader asks for a total of 10 points.

Musical Hugs

Age Appeal:	Grades K-5

Purpose:	Social interaction and group cooperation
Equipment:	Lively music
Group Size:	Any size
Setting:	Gym or outdoors

DESCRIPTION: Participants move around play area walking to the beat of the music. When the music stops, each player hugs a partner. When the music begins again, everyone walks again. When music stops next, players hug in groups of 3. Play continues with participants adding one more person each time the music stops, until finally the entire group is together in one big hug!

One Behind

Age Appeal:	Grades K-5

Purpose:	General strength and endurance
Equipment:	Lively music
Group Size:	Any size
Setting:	Gym or outdoors

DESCRIPTION: This is a fun memory game where the students are challenged to remember a certain movement and repeat it. The teacher or leader stands facing the group in a place where all can see. The leader does an action (running in place, doing half jacks, curl-ups, push-ups, etc.) or strikes a pose (arms in air, hands on hips, etc.) The group watches this action. When the leader does a second action or pose, the group begins by doing the first action or pose. The group continues until the leader does a third action or pose. The group then performs the second one. Play continues with the group always one action behind the leader. Music is played during this activity.

Teacher Tip:	• This is a great activity for "warm-up" movements, demonstrating and practicing movement patterns (pivot, sliding, galloping) and dance steps (step-hop, 2-step, heel-toe).

Elastic Stretch

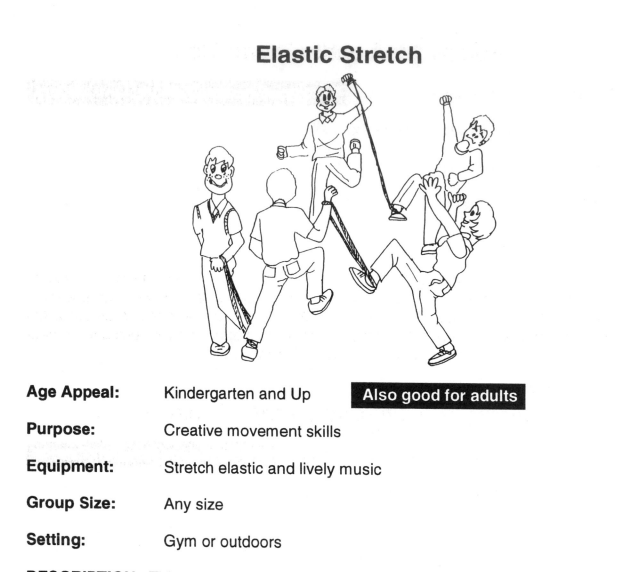

Age Appeal: Kindergarten and Up   **Also good for adults**

Purpose: Creative movement skills

Equipment: Stretch elastic and lively music

Group Size: Any size

Setting: Gym or outdoors

DESCRIPTION: This activity uses teacher-made lengths of stretch elastic that have been tied at each end to form a loop large enough for wrists and ankles. The stretch elastic can be purchased from a fabric shop. The participant loops the elastic around one wrist and the opposite ankle. The elastic should be taut, but not over-stretched. To begin, everyone is scattered about the playing area and lively music is played. Participants move creatively, making as many different poses and movements as possible. The teacher or leader can suggest ways to move---changing levels, directions, traveling, etc. After a few minutes of moving alone, participants pair up with another person. Couples exchange wrist loops and then continue moving creatively, keeping the elastic taut.

The activity continues with each couple joining with another pair. They share wrist loops and this group of four players moves to the music. This process of grouping continues while the music plays until the entire group is linked together. At the end, all participants strike an ending pose and freeze for a few seconds. Afterward, each person removes the wrist band, lets it drop, and walks out from the group to untangle the elastic.

Teacher Tip: The stretch elastic can be any width, but the wider type (men's pajama elastic) seems to work the best.

Follow the Leader Warm-Ups

Age Appeal: Kindergarten and Up   **Also good for teens, adults, and seniors**

Purpose: Cardiovascular fitness

Equipment: Lively music

Group Size: Any size

Setting: Gym or outdoors

DESCRIPTION: An effective way to prepare a group for active participation in a class or party is through movement designed to increase the heart rate and warm up the muscles. Accompanied by some lively music with a 4/4 beat, the leader can create a fun and exciting workout experience. Movements range from familiar calisthenics to maneuvers with small equipment such as wands, ribbons, jump ropes, etc.

Mops, Towels, and Carpet Squares

Age Appeal: Kindergarten to Fourth Grade   **Also good for teens and adults**

Purpose: Cardiovascular fitness

Equipment: Lively music

Group Size: Any size

Setting: Gym with a smooth wooden floor

DESCRIPTION: Here are a few fun ways to use "recycled" materials for a nonstop musical treat! Lively music is played while the teacher directs the students with the following activities:

Mop Skates: These are made by attaching 2 pieces of rope cording to the back of an old mop head. The students tie the mops on by wrapping the cord around back of the ankle and at the top of the foot. If the student's feet are too big to fit into the mop opening, just insert the front part of the foot. Each student uses two mop heads to "skate."

Towels and Carpet Squares: Each person has a bath-size towel. The towel is placed on the floor and the students stand on it. This activity is like "Follow The Leader," as the students follow the movements directed by the leader. A similar activity can be done using carpet squares. Each person has a carpet square. By placing their hands on an upside down carpet square, the players can push it around the floor. By standing on the carpet, twisting and scooting movements can be done. As with the towels, movement ideas are as varied as the imagination of the participants and leaders.

Slide and Count

Age Appeal: Fourth Grade and Up   <mark>**Also good for teens and adults**</mark>

Purpose: Cardiovascular fitness, basic timing skills

Equipment: Lively music

Group Size: Any size

Setting: Gym or outdoors

DESCRIPTION: This activity is aerobically challenging and mentally engaging! Direct the students to form a double circle formation. The students face toward the center and hold hands with the person on each side. When the music begins, those students in the outside circle slide to the left, while those in the inside circle slide to the right. This sliding action is done in a certain pattern:

- 16 counts in first direction, then 16 counts in the opposite direction
- 8 counts in first direction, then 8 counts in the opposite direction
- 4 counts in first direction, then 4 counts in the opposite direction
- 2 counts in first direction, then 2 counts in the opposite direction
- Repeat all of the above until the end of the music

Teacher Tips: Use music with a steady 4/4 beat that is appropriate for a sliding action. A fun variation is to have the inside circle move first and then "freeze," while the outside circle moves. In this variation, the inside circle moves and then is copied by the other circle.

Paper Dancing

Great for a "Rainy Day"

Age Appeal: Third Grade and Up   **Also good for teens, adults, and seniors**

Purpose: Creative movement skills

Equipment: One piece of recycled 8-1/2" x 11" paper per person and lively music

Group Size: Any size

Setting: Gym, classroom or outdoors

DESCRIPTION: This is a great way to recycle used sheets of paper. The teacher stands facing the class. The teacher and all of the students have a piece of paper. Music is played while the group follows a series of movements made with the paper by the leader. Here is a sample sequence:

A. Begin by holding the paper with two hands and fan the paper slowly, then faster.

B. Hold the paper with one hand and fan. Hold the paper with the other hand and fan.

C. Crunch up paper slowly in one hand, toss and catch the paper ball. Throw the paper ball high into the air, turn around, and then catch it.

D. Slowly try to uncrinkle the paper ball with one hand; then use other hand to help until the sheet is in the original shape.

E. Put the paper on the floor and jump across it, to each side, and on top of it. Pick the paper sheet up, and wave it to bring the activity to a close.

Pass the Leadership for Fitness

Age Appeal: Third Grade and Up   **Also good for teens and adults**

Purpose: Cardiovascular fitness

Equipment: Lively music

Group Size: Any size

Setting: Gym or outdoors

DESCRIPTION: The group stands in a circle with all of the students facing inward. As music begins, one person starts leading the group in a sustained movement. For example, marching in place. After about 30 seconds, the leader cups both hands together and passes the imaginary leadership "magic" to the person standing to the leader's right. Without any dialogue, the next person begins leading and others follow. This creative movement activity continues as each person has a chance to be the leader.

Teacher Tips:

- It is easier to lead and to follow the movements if the pace of the music is slow and the movements are also performed in a slow and sustained manner.

- Remind the leaders to perform the movements so that the participants can retain eye contact with them. The movements should be repeated a few times before changing to a new movement.

- The leaders should be encouraged to do something that has not already been performed.

Funny Faces

Age Appeal: Third Grade and Up   **Also good for teens, adults, and seniors**

Purpose: Social interaction and interpersonal skills

Equipment: Bags of cotton balls,
bottles of hand lotion,
small balls, and lively music

Group Size: Any size

Setting: Gym, classroom, or outdoors

Great for a "Rainy Day"

DESCRIPTION: Divide the class into groups of 8-10 players. Each group sits in a circle formation with all of the players facing the center. A small ball (or other appropriate object) is passed from person to person around the circle. Music is played as the ball is being passed. The ball must be handed (not thrown), and must be accepted by the next player. The object is to not get caught with the ball when the music stops. When the music stops, the player with the ball receives a forfeit.

Each group has a "forfeit giver" standing outside and near the circle. This person should have a supply of cotton balls and small bottles of hand lotion. When the music stops, the helper places a dab of lotion on the nose (or other part of the face) of the "caught" player, and immediately sticks a cotton ball on the lotion. If a player is caught more than once, additional cotton balls are applied to the face.

Play continues for 10-12 rounds. At the end of the game, most of the students should have one or more of these "warm fuzzies" on their faces! The game is really a blast! If you have a camera, a group picture taken of all players with cotton balls on their faces is a neat addition to this activity.

Crazy Musical Hot Potato

Age Appeal: Third Grade and Up   **Also good for teens and adults**

Purpose: Social interaction and general coordination skills

Equipment: Balloons and lively music

Group Size: Any size

Setting: Gym or outdoors

DESCRIPTION: Divide the class into smaller groups of 6-8 players. The players in each group are seated in a circle, facing the center. Each group is given an inflated balloon. When the music is played, the balloon is continually handed from one player to the next around the circle. The balloon should be passed in only one direction and must be accepted when passed. Play continues until the music stops. The player holding the balloon when the music stops must complete a fun challenge which is announced at that point by the teacher. The challenge must be performed by that person each time he receives the balloon for the remainder of the game. Sample challenges could be:

1. Stand up and yell, "Whoopee" then sit and pass the balloon to the next player.

2. Pass the balloon around your body before passing it to the next player.

3. Pass the balloon under both legs before passing it to the next player.

4. Bat the balloon into the air two times before passing it to the next player.

After the challenge is announced, the game immediately resumes (music begins again). If, when the music stops, a different group member is holding the balloon, he will perform the first challenge. If a group member is caught for a second time, a new, additional challenge is announced and both are performed by that person.

For instance, a person in the group who has been "caught" three times, would need to:

1. Stand and yell, "Whoopee,"

2. Pass the balloon around his body,

3. Pass the balloon under his legs---before handing the balloon to the next player.

Teacher Tips:

- The leader can often control the music so that many different players will get caught.

- A soft object, rather than a balloon, can be used for passing, but balloons add an element of "fun" to this game.

- Players might need to be reminded to pass the balloon, not bat the balloon.

"Pass the Shoe" Challenge

Age Appeal: Third Grade and Up | Also good for teens, adults, and seniors |

Purpose: Group cooperation and general coordination skills

Equipment: None

Group Size: Any size

Setting: Gym

DESCRIPTION: Divide the class into smaller groups of 6-8 players. Each group sits in a circle formation with all of the players facing the center. Every student takes off one shoe. The object of this singing game is for the players to pass the shoes around the circle in a counterclockwise direction while singing and exchanging shoes on a specific beat. The words to the song are:

Words:	Actions:
"You must <u>pass</u> this <u>shoe</u>..." "From me to <u>you</u>, to <u>you</u>,...." "You must <u>pass</u> this <u>shoe</u>..." "And do just as I <u>do</u>."	Pass the shoe on each underlined word Pass the shoe on each underlined word Pass the shoe on each underlined word On the first "do," tap the shoe on the floor on the right side, then back on the left side on the words "just as I," and then pass it on the underlined "do."

The shoe is held during the taps, which take place directly in front, slightly right, then left. Once players have learned the song and played several practice rounds, challenge each of the groups to see if they can play the game without any mistakes for at least three rounds.

Balloon Keep-It-Up

Age Appeal: Fourth Grade and Up   **Also good for teens and adults**

Purpose: Group cooperation and general coordination skills

Equipment: Large round balloons and lively music

Group Size: Any size

Setting: Gym

DESCRIPTION: Divide your class into groups of 6-8 players. Each group forms a circle by standing and holding hands. Each group inflates and ties off a large, round balloon. When the music begins, players bat the balloon into the air. The object is to keep the balloon from hitting the floor. The balloon can be batted with <u>any</u> body part during the first round.

If a group "goofs" (balloon hits floor or hands break apart) the group should sit down and continue playing. After a minute or two, the music is stopped and the teacher calls out that the round has ended. Groups still standing receive 1,000 points. The directions are given for the second round and play begins again as the music starts. There are several rounds to this activity, and directions are listed as follows:

80

- Round 1 - Players in each group can use any body part, but must keep their hands together. If a group "goofs," the group sits down and continues playing. Winning groups receive 1,000 points.

- Round 2 - Continue to hold hands, but balloon must be batted with body parts other than the hands and arms. Players may use their head, shoulders, knees, and feet. Winning groups receive 2,000 points.

- Round 3 - During this round, the players begin by sitting on the floor in a circle. Hands and arms may be used, but hands must stay clasped. If a group "goofs" they stand up and continue playing. Award 3,000 points to any group that is still sitting.

- Round 4 - Players lie on their backs with their heads in towards the center. (The players look like spokes of a large wheel.) They hold hands and may use them and all other body parts to keep the balloon from hitting the floor. A short practice time could be given before actual play begins. This is the hardest round, so two "goofs" might be permitted before the group sits up and plays as in Round 3. Award 4,000 points to any group that is still lying down.

Teacher Tips:
- All rounds should end when most groups have "goofed" or after a 2-minute period, whichever happens first. It is fine to have several winning groups each round.

- While we give points during this activity, it is really not important to the activity. We announce the score after each round just for fun.

- This activity emphasizes cooperation while engaged in a fun competitive situation. No participant is ever eliminated, so a "goof" just means the task is changed.

Race Track

Age Appeal: Grades K-3

Purpose: Physical strength and endurance

Equipment: Cue cards and lively music

Group Size: Any size

Setting: Gym

DESCRIPTION: The play area is set up to resemble a race track, with space for running on the outside area. The center of the area is designated as the Gas Station where children can stop to rest. Spaced between the Gas Station and the Track, at intervals, are large cards on which a set of directions have been written. These cards represent Pit Stops. Each card gives information and direction about exercise actions, and each card is different:

• **UNDER THE HOOD:**	Students perform curl-ups on the mats.
• **PUMPING:**	Students perform half-jacks or jump rope at this station.
• **RACING MOTOR:**	Students jog in place---knees high.
• **WINDSHIELD WIPERS:**	Students swing outstretched arms across and in back of their body.
• **WHEEL ROTATION:**	Students sit in a chair and "bicycle" legs in the air.
• **MOTOR TUNE UP:**	Students are on all fours -- hands and feet -- and kick one leg up, then the other.

Before the Activity Begins: The children are familiarized with the terms, exercise actions and guidelines for playing. As a group, they will visit each Pit Stop and observe a demonstration of each exercise. Safety standards are also discussed:

- Pass another racing car on the inside.
- Be sure to sound your horn before passing.
- If you need to get gas (rest), slow your car down before cutting into the "infield".

How to Play: Divide children into six groups and make sure they know who is in their group. Each group starts at one of the six exercise stations to begin this activity. The teacher announces that the race is about to start, "Students start your engines. Go!"

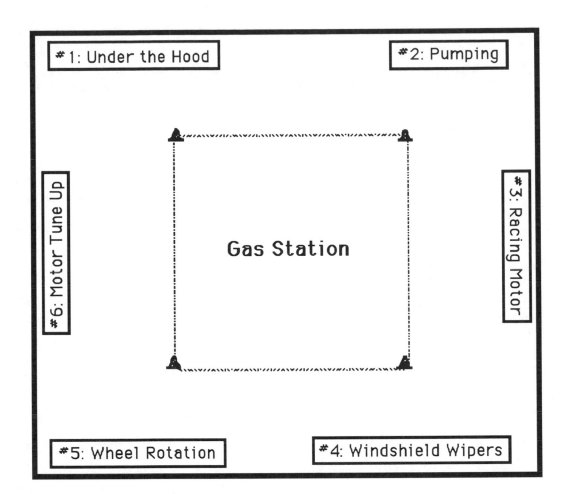

The students run around the track. Any time the teacher calls out "Pit Stop," the group must come together at their original starting station and immediately begin the exercise written on that card, and continue until the teachers calls, "All race cars back on the track!" With this cue, the students continue around the track. When the teacher calls out "Pit Stop!" again, each group moves on to the next exercise station. This continues until each group has visited each Pit Stop.

Teacher Tips:	•	The use of appropriate music and simulated voice projection (to sound like race track announcer) enhances this activity.
	•	This activity can be modified for use with younger students. Since younger children may forget where the "next" station is located, they do best to either just run around the track and come into the center to rest and "gas up," or not run around, but just visit each Pit Stop.

A Boy, A Rope and a Truth

By Elam R. Hill, Former Director of Physical Education
Sequoia Junior High School, Fresno, California

Today I saw truth. For a moment I lived and breathed in the great presence of truth and felt its sweetness plunge deep into my soul. I am a teacher and coach in a junior high school. I work with over 500 boys each day. This has been my occupation for over 20 years. I enjoy it. Traditionally, I am supposed to be rugged, tough, crusty; yes, even a little severe at times ... and yet, underneath this exterior, feeling and understanding must exist if the job is to be done.

Today was test day in climbing the rope. We climb from a standing start to a point 15 feet high. One of my tasks these past few weeks has been to train and teach the boys to negotiate this distance in as few seconds as possible. The school record for this event is 2.1 seconds. It has stood for three years. Today this record was broken. But this is not my story. How this record was broken is the important thing here. As it so often is in many an endeavor in this life.

For three years Bobby Polacio, a 14-1/2 year-old ninth grade Mexican-American boy, has trained and pointed, and, I suspect, dreamed of breaking this record. It has been his consuming passion; it seems his whole life depended upon breaking this record.

In his first of three attempts Bobby climbed the rope in 2.1 seconds, tying the record. In the second try the watch stopped at 2.0 seconds flat, a record! But, as he descended the rope and the entire class gathered around to check the watch, I knew I must ask Bobby a question. There was a slight doubt in my mind whether or not the board at the 15 foot height had been touched. If he had missed, it was so very, very, close -- not more than a fraction of an inch -- and only Bobby knew this answer.

As he walked toward me, expressionless, I said. "Bobby, did you touch?" If he had said "Yes" the record he had dreamed of since he was a skinny seventh grader and had worked for almost daily would be his, and he knew I would trust his word. With the class already cheering him for his performance, the slim, brown-skinned boy shook his head negatively. And in this simple gesture, I witnessed a moment of greatness.

Coaches do not cry. Only babies cry, they say. But as I reached out to pat this boy on the shoulder, there was a small drop of water in each eye. And it was with effort, through a tight throat, that I told the class: "This boy has not set a record in the rope climb. No, he has set a much finer record, a real genuine record for you and me and everyone to strive for. He has told the simple truth."

I turned to Bobby and said, "Bobby, I'm proud of you. You've just set a record many athletes never attain. Now, in your last try, I want you to jump a few inches higher on the take off. You're going to break this record."

After the other boys had finished their next turns and Bobby came up to the rope for his last try, a strange stillness came over the gymnasium. Fifty boys and one coach were breathlessly set to help boost Bobby Polacio to a new record. He climbed the rope in 1.9 seconds!

When the bell rang and I walked away, now misty-eyed from this group of boys, I was thinking... "Bobby, with your brown skin, with your clear, bright, dark eyes and your straight trim body -- Bobby at age 14 you are a better man than I. Thank you for climbing so very, very high today."

More Thoughts on Student Behavior: Misconduct is often a cry for attention. Sometimes children (and adults) are accustomed to being the center of attention, and they continue to seek this in a group setting. When a person lacks the skill to do a requested action (bat a ball, etc.) he will often try to cover up an inadequacy with inappropriate behavior. When the leader/teacher identifies either of these as a probable cause, steps must be taken to rechannel such actions. There are times when it would be best to merely ignore a minor disruption. Once again, if the misconduct is of short duration and not a safety issue, drawing attention to it might prove to be more disruptive to the class.

Use Finesse: It is important, although not a natural reaction, for the leader/teacher to handle these situations with finesse and diplomacy. To do otherwise will only aggravate and magnify the problem. After years of teaching, I can only say that <u>no single or definite solution</u> can be offered to solve every off-task student behavioral problem. However, here are three strategies to consider:

#1 Give the student a different task or a new position in the game. This type of redirection may prove to be helpful.

#2 Just ignore the behavior for the time being and/or make a few positive comments to the students in close proximity to the student who is misbehaving. Often students who are off-task will get back "on-track" when they see other students receiving praise from the teacher.

#3 At some time during the rest of the class period, catch the student in the act of doing something positive. Comment on this to the student to reinforce his or her positive behavior.

Consider the Environment: The playing area and the equipment can be sources of distraction and can trigger disturbances. Children arriving at a gym or playground after being in a classroom setting for several hours will naturally be stimulated. Even equipment may immediately focus attention away from the leader/teacher. You may want to:

- Allow a few minutes for free play (in the area and with equipment) before formal instruction begins.
- In a larger-than-needed play area, set boundaries with cones, ropes, etc. to designate a smaller area.
- Design activities that require no equipment until a learning environment has been established.
- Hand out equipment after instructions have been given and understood.
- Use minimum equipment first, and then add more later.

4 Small Group Games:
"Fun Fireworks for All!"

Chapter Overview: This chapter contains a fun selection of games and activities that can be used with small groups or by dividing the class into smaller groups. The activities will help to build and develop teamwork and group cooperation skills, and will enhance social interaction.

Discipline Tip #4: Key Ingredients

In my observations of classroom teachers, physical education teachers, and recreation leaders during my professional career, I have "discovered" a key ingredient for success. I have seen it help students to blossom, lift the spirit of inner-city youth, and bring about dramatic changes in the lives of student-athletes. Do you know what it is?

It helps to transform a "dead" classroom into a high achieving one. It will help you to be more productive and self-satisfied. This key ingredient helps to make a good teacher better and a better teacher, the best! Getting this key ingredient sometimes takes years of experience, sometimes not. Here it is. Are you ready? The key ingredient is called "knowing and understanding your students." Here is an assortment of truths about kids and teaching:

- Kids want you to know their names. Learn them!

- Kids are interested in the process. Adults usually are more interested in the end product. So praise their <u>progress</u>, as well as the results of their efforts!

- It takes as much energy for a child to stand still as it does for adults to move. Think about it!

- Kids like to hear good things about themselves. Take time to say something positive to each child every day!

- Parents like to hear good things about their kids too. Call parents and tell them that you enjoy their child!

- And lastly, kids don't have to be looking at you all the time to be listening.

The Giant Calculator

Age Appeal: Grades 1-4

Purpose: Math skills

Equipment: Math flash cards and a "giant calculator."

Group Size: For small groups of two to four players

Setting: Outdoors

DESCRIPTION: A giant calculator, similar to the one shown below, is made by using chalk on an outdoor surface. The calculator can be permanently painted onto an outdoor playing area in the same manner as a hopscotch design:

ON/OFF	7	8	9
X	4	5	6
+	1	2	3
−	÷	=	0

In this game, the players take turns trying to correctly solve the math flash cards. A player is shown a card and then solves the problem by jumping or hopping on the giant calculator. Cards with math oriented problems can be drawn up for players to use. The difficulty of the problems would be dependent on the ages of the players. Here is an example for a student using basic addition:

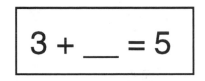

To correctly answer this question, the student would have to perform the following:

1. Hop or jump onto the "on" space
2. Hop or jump onto the "3" space
3. Hop or jump onto the "+" (plus) space
4. Hop or jump onto the "2" space
5. Hop or jump onto the "=" (equals) space
6. Hop or jump onto the "5" space
7. Hop or jump onto the "off" space
8. Hop or jump off of the calculator

If this is correctly executed, that player would get one point. A new math flash card would be shown to the next player. The other players help to check the accuracy of the student's responses. Whether or not a player is in error, when accidentally stepping on a line, can be decided by the player with the flash cards. Emphasis might be on getting the answer correct, rather than on touching a line while jumping.

Variation: Another game which is fun to play with the "Calculator" is similar to "Twister." This game can be played as singles or with a partner. As singles, one player reads the problem and responds using different body parts (hand, foot, knee, elbow, etc.) to complete the answer. For example, with "8+7=__ ," the player answers the problem by:

1. Left foot steps on the "on" space
2. Right foot steps on the "8" space
3. Right hand is placed on the "+" space
4. Right foot steps on the "7" space
5. Right hand is placed on the "=" space
6. Left foot steps on the "1" space and the right foot on the "5" space
7. Right hand is placed on the "off" space
8. Jump off of the calculator

Any time a number is a double digit, the player places two body parts on the calculator at one time. This game is even more fun when played as doubles or in a small group. Players take turns placing a body part in a correct square. Once a body part is placed, it cannot be moved unless it would be impossible to complete the problem otherwise.

All Aboard

Age Appeal: Second grade and Up   **Also good for teens and adults**

Purpose: Group problem-solving and cooperation skills

Equipment: Square 2' x 2' pieces of plywood

Group Size: For small groups of eight to ten players

Setting: Gym or outdoors

DESCRIPTION: The object of this activity is for all members of the small group to stand on the 2' x 2' plywood board without anyone touching the ground. The players must hold this formation for 10 seconds. Play begins as soon as the directions are given and is over when the "challenge" has been solved.

Teacher Tip: When the group has accomplished the formation, have them sing a song like "Row, Row, Row Your Boat" instead of holding the formation for 10 seconds.

Variations:
- Challenge the group to add more people.

- Use two groups (16 to 20 players) by placing two "All Aboards" together.

- Allow no one to speak.

- Require both feet to be in contact with the wooden surface. This is ideal with smaller groups of players.

Beach Ball Challenges

Age Appeal: Third grade and Up   **Also good for teens and adults**

Purpose: Problem-solving and cooperation skills

Equipment: Beach balls

Group Size: Partners

Setting: Gym or outdoors

DESCRIPTION: This activity is designed to challenge partners to complete tasks while keeping a beach ball positioned between designated body parts without using hands. Traveling from one place to another or performing a particular stunt is usually included in the challenge.

Challenges Can Include:

- Carry the beach ball using your heads.

- Carry the beach ball using your sides.

- Carry the beach ball using your stomach.

- Carry the beach ball back to back, or head to back, or stomach to back.

- From a kneeling position, lift the beach ball with your heads until you are standing.

- From a lying position, lift the beach ball with your heads until you are standing.

Other Ideas:

- Travel through an obstacle course with your partner.

- Hop, slide, gallop, or skip to travel.

- Move apart then quickly back together before the ball hits the ground.

Bump

Age Appeal: Fourth grade and Up   **Also good for teens and adults**

Purpose: Cooperation skills

Equipment: Soft foam ball or foam frisbee, hula hoop

Group Size: For groups of three players

Setting: Gym or outdoors

DESCRIPTION: Two players stand back-to-back about fifteen feet away from the third player. The two players are called the "Catchers". The third member of the group has a soft frisbee or foam ball and is called the "Thrower". A hula hoop is placed in an area about 5 feet behind the Throwers. Several teams can use the same hula hoop.

On a signal to start, the Thrower tosses the frisbee so it can be caught by the two team mates. The Catchers may not use their hands or arms, but must catch the frisbee between their bodies. If a throw is not legitimately caught, the frisbee is quickly returned to the Thrower, who continues to throw until an acceptable catch is made. When this occurs, the Catchers travel with the frisbee pressed tightly between them (still without the use of hands or arms), and deposit it into the hoop.

If the frisbee is dropped en route or in the process of being dropped in, players quickly return to the starting line and begin again. If the frisbee is successfully deposited, one of the Catchers becomes the Thrower, and the game continues. When all three members of the group have been a successful Thrower, the game is over. At this point, all three players would have all been successful at throwing, catching, traveling, and depositing.

Folf - Frisbee Golf

Age Appeal: Third grade and Up   **Also good for teens and adults**

Purpose: Frisbee throwing skills

Equipment: Frisbees

Group Size: For groups of 2-4 players

Setting: Outdoors

DESCRIPTION: Folf, another name for Frisbee Golf, can be played outdoors almost anywhere. Players in a group compete against each other by throwing a frisbee at predetermined objects (bushes, lamp posts, trees, fire hydrants, etc.) as they advance from one object to another. The goal is to throw the frisbee as few times as possible in route to each location (hole) and to finish the entire course with the lowest score (the winner).

The distance between "holes" varies according to throwing skills of the participants, the available playing area, and the restraints of class control that might be necessary. Players can set their own "holes" so that they can jog between throws and incorporate an aerobic component into the game. Players can agree on "holes" as they play (after recording the score, they can look around and decide on the next "hole") or a predetermined course can be set up and marked by numbers. Players would throw from one hole to the next in sequence.

Gotcha!

Age Appeal: Fourth Grade and Up

Also good for teens and adults

Purpose: General body management skills

Equipment: None

Group Size: For groups of 8-12 players

Setting: Gym or outdoors

Great for a "Rainy Day"

DESCRIPTION: The players stand in a large circle, facing inward. One player "IT" stands in the center. On a signal given by IT, the players attempt to move without being seen by IT. The object of the game is to move from a standing position to a lying position, and then back to a standing position without being seen by IT.

The players move only when they think IT is not looking. Their movements must be quick and deliberate, with the players quickly "freezing" so that they are not seen by IT when they are moving. If they can successfully do this without being caught by IT, they win. The winner will then trade places with IT, and a new game begins.

Any time that IT spots a moving person, he points to that person and says, "Gotcha." When this happens, the player who was spotted starts again from the standing position. There can be no arguing or disputing, if IT says a person was moving, that person must begin again.

Teacher Tips:	• During play, all participants are moving, pausing, and progressing at the same time. IT is turning, pointing, yelling "Gotcha" and constantly trying to spot someone moving.
	• This is a rapidly moving game and players improve after a few minutes of participation.
	• The game is not always easy to explain. A short demonstration is always helpful.

Tangle

Age Appeal: Fifth Grade and Up   **Also good for teens and adults**

Purpose: Group cooperation and problem-solving skills

Equipment: None

Group Size: For groups of 8-10 players

Setting: Gym or outdoors

DESCRIPTION: Players stand in a circle facing inward and extend both arms into the center. At random, each person grasps hands with two different people on the opposite side of the circle. To play, the group works together to untangle into a single circle without letting go of any hands. A contest can be held between groups to accomplish the task in the shortest period of time. However, guidelines might determine that all groups finishing within a prescribed time frame are all winners.

Teacher Tips: If an impossible-to-untangle situation occurs, instruct the group to decide on one "operation" which allows one pair of hands to be unclasped, moved as needed, and then reclasped as play continues. If appropriate, points can be deducted from a group that requires an "operation" in order to solve the activity.

Variations: Instead of grasping hands, each participant can hold a short length of rope or a recycled panty hose "leg" in one hand. The game is then played the same way as described above. This method assures more movement and adds a different element to the activity.

Hunker Down

Age Appeal: Third Grade and Up   **Also good for teens**

Purpose: General body management skills

Equipment: A long jump rope, carpet squares

Group Size: For partners

Setting: Gym or outdoors

DESCRIPTION: The partners squat (hunker down) on top of carpet squares about ten feet apart. Each partner holds the end of a long jump rope. Partners are facing each other. On a signal to start, they pull or "slack up" on the rope in an attempt to unbalance the other person, while retaining their own balance.

A player is considered unbalanced if he stands up, loses his grip on the rope, or falls off the base. One point is awarded to the winner, and several predetermined rounds are played. The person with the highest score is the winner.

100 Feet of String

Age Appeal: Kindergarten and Up   **Also good for teens, adults, and seniors**

Purpose: Group cooperation and teamwork skills

Equipment: Varied lengths of string or yarn, 75-100 pieces

95

Group Size: Small groups of 2-4 players. **Note:** This is a fun inter-generational game. You can have one child, one teen, one adult, and one senior per team!

Setting: Anywhere

DESCRIPTION: Approximately 75-100 pieces of yarn or string, varying in length from one foot to several feet are hidden and/or scattered within the playing area prior to game time. Participants are divided into teams.

On a signal to start, players collect and tie together as many pieces of string as possible during a 5 minute period. The object is for a team to have the longest length when time is called. At the end of the game, a stopping signal should be sounded, and no more tying should be done. Lengths of string are then stretched out on the ground for measuring, and a winning team is declared.

> **Teacher Tips:** Several pieces of colored string can be considered "magic." When determining the final length, this magic string can add 5' to the team's score.

Balloon Rocket Relay

Age Appeal: Fourth Grade and Up   **Also good for teens and adults**

Purpose: Group cooperation and teamwork skills

Equipment: One balloon per player

Group Size: For small groups of 2-4 players

Setting: Gym or outdoors

DESCRIPTION: Teams of 2 to 4 players gather behind a starting line. Each player has a balloon. On a signal to start, one player from each team inflates a balloon (to any size) and throws it forward. The balloon will zig and zag around as the air escapes. The second team member will then kneel on top of that balloon, inflate his balloon, stand up and throw it. Play continues as team members take turns towards a finish line. If playing in a gym, the wall at the far end of the gym could be the finish line. Once a balloon has been thrown and hits the wall, all of the team members quickly run back to the starting point and sit down.

> **Teacher Tips:** This social recreation type game promotes a lot of laughter. The process of "just playing" is superior to that of winning and should be emphasized. This game can be played in a short period of time, usually 2-3 minutes.

Slow Motion Sports

Age Appeal: Kindergarten and Up   Also good for teens and adults

Purpose: Creative movement skills

Equipment: None

Group Size: For small groups of 2-3 players

Setting: Gym or outdoors

DESCRIPTION: The participants work in small groups or with a partner. Each group moves in slow motion to act out a specific sport, as suggested by the teacher or leader.

Sports might be:
- Karate
- Boxing
- Baseball
- Tennis
- Wrestling

The partners or small group members move in an action-reaction manner. For example, if the game was baseball, one person pitches an imaginary ball (in slow motion, of course). After a short delay (while imaginary ball travels), the second player swings at the ball and misses. The third player is the umpire and calls a "strike!" This continues until the batter hits a home run. All three players watch the "ball" travel to the grandstands. After several sports have been experienced, each group is asked to pick one to share with the other members of the class.

Towel Toss

Age Appeal: Third Grade and Up   Also good for teens and adults

Purpose: Cooperation skills

Equipment: Towels and playground balls

Group Size: For small groups of 4 players

Setting: Gym or outdoors

DESCRIPTION: The teams of four scatter about the playing area. Each player holds two corners of a bath-size towel (two people hold one towel). The object of this game is to toss a playground ball from one towel to the other pair's towel. In this manner, the ball is thrown and caught back and forth between the two partners. The throwing

distance should be short to begin with and increase as players become more proficient. Throwing height can also be increased and improved with practice.

This activity can be transformed into a competitive game by staging a contest between teams for successful distance throwing. The leader/teacher can suggest: "See how many times your team can throw and catch the ball successfully (not letting it touch the ground) before I call time."

Teacher Tip: If you do not have enough playground balls, a large foam ball or a volleyball is ideal in weight and size for this activity.

Bring Me An Object

Age Appeal: Kindergarten and Up

Also good for teens, adults, and seniors

Great for a "Rainy Day"

Purpose: Social interaction and teamwork skills

Equipment: A list of objects, pen and
paper for keeping score

Group Size: For small groups of 4-6 players

Setting: Gym, classroom, or outdoors

DESCRIPTION: The small groups of 4-6 players are seated together, equal distance from the leader who is located in front of the participants. The leader has a prepared list of items and a score keeping card or board. Teams are named (or numbered) and each team selects a Runner.

To play, the leader calls out a specific item. The Runner attempts to gain this item from a teammate and take it to the leader before other team Runners can do so. The first Runner to reach the leader with the correct item scores a point for their team. If the item describes a person in the group (For example, "someone wearing braces" or "a person who has a baby brother under one year old"), then the Runner holds hands with that person and brings him to the leader to score the point. The object of the game is to score the most points during playing time. A game might last 10-15 minutes. A list of 25-30 items should be prepared before the game is played.

Teacher Tips:	•	A creative list of objects best suited to reflect students in your class will add to the fun and success of this game. Suggestions:

    1. a white sock with a hole in it

    2. four belts hooked together

    3. a ring with a blue stone

    4. a person who bites his or her fingernails

    5. someone who was born west of the Mississippi River

    6. a coin dated earlier than 1985

    7. a picture of someone's mother

More Teacher Tips:	• A different Runner can be selected midway through the game.
	• The method of traveling to the leader can be changed for each round to add another dimension to the game. For example, the Runner may have to skip, jump, or gallop to get to the leader.
	• Emphasize that only the Runner, or a Runner holding hands with a team member, can successfully score.

Communication Challenge

Age Appeal: Fourth Grade and Up   **Also good for teens, adults, and seniors**

Purpose: Communication/language arts skills

Equipment: Wooden blocks or pieces of cardboard, diagram sheets, extra sheets of paper and pencils

Group Size: For small groups of 2-4 players

Setting: Gym or classroom

Great for a "Rainy Day"

DESCRIPTION: Groups assemble together around a small table or are seated on the floor. Each group should have a set of 5 cardboard or wooden blocks similar in size and shape to those drawn on the next page. The sheet has drawings for 5 rounds of this activity. The object is for one person to verbally describe a configuration while a second player assembles the description using the blocks. The two players sit back to back (or so they cannot see what each other is doing.) Observers (non-players in the group) position themselves to watch, and wait a turn. This is how the game is played:

A. The describer looks at the first diagram and tells the person with the rectangles how to place them in relation to each other to duplicate the drawing.

B. The listener arranges the blocks as described and then asks an observer to draw what has been arranged.

C. The players switch positions for the next diagram.

Teacher Tip: If you have a limited amount of time, the teacher or leader can describe the diagrams while the other four players (without looking at each other's work), draw what is described.

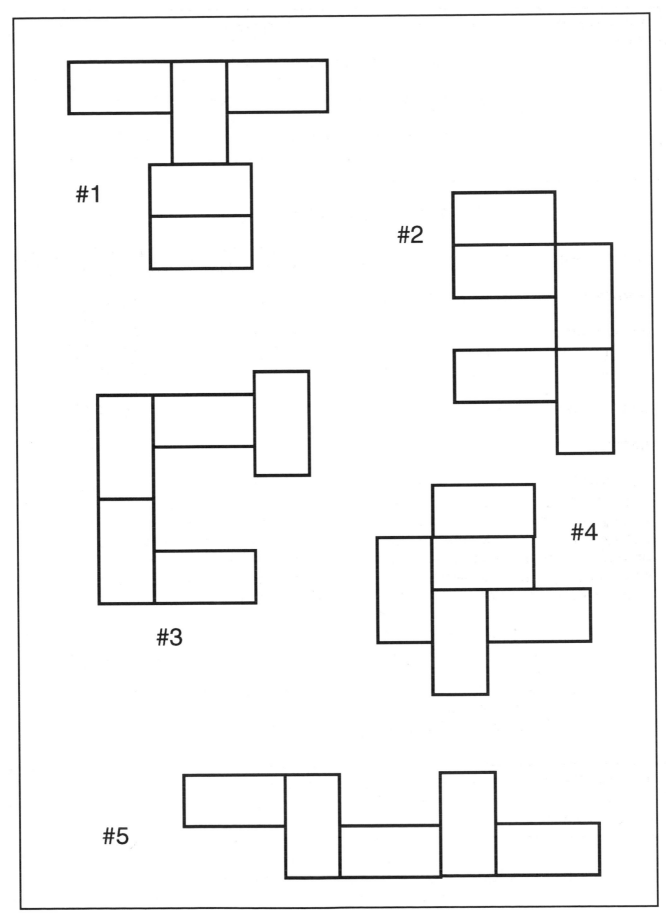

#1

#2

#3

#4

#5

Draw It Charades

Age Appeal: Third Grade and Up

Also good for teens, adults, and seniors

Purpose: Problem-solving skills

Equipment: List of song titles, paper and magic marker

Group Size: For small groups of 4-6 players

Setting: Anywhere

Great for a "Rainy Day"

DESCRIPTION: The members in each group are huddled close together with blank paper and a magic marker. One member of the group goes to the teacher, who is located in a central place in the room. When all groups are represented, the teacher whispers the title of a song to them. They return to their group, position their paper and pen for drawing, and await the teacher's signal to begin.

The object of the game is for the group's representative to draw the song title so that the other members of the group can guess the song. The person drawing may not speak, hum, gesture, use letters or numbers, or in any way aid the "guessers" except by drawing a picture.

When the group does arrive at the correct answer, they sing the song or hum the tune. At this point, the round is over and other groups stop. Each group writes the correct song title on the paper, and the winning group also adds a star (*). This drawing is set aside for future viewing and enjoyment.

The game continues as a new group representative approaches the leader for another song title. Six or more rounds should be played, and every team member should have a turn as "the artist". The teacher has a concealed list of song titles, which has been prepared before game time. Careful thought should be given to the title selection so that some are easy ("Mary Had A Little Lamb") and others are difficult ("William Tell Overture"). It is wise to have 15-20 titles, just in case more songs are needed.

Teacher Tips: • The leader should emphasize and enforce the starting time so that all groups begin together.

• At the conclusion of the game, it is fun to display all the pictures and to see the many different ways the same song title was depicted. The star (*) helps recall the winner.

• It might be necessary to remind players of the no-hints or helping rules.

The Dinner Party

Age Appeal: Third Grade and Up   <mark>Also good for teens, adults, and seniors</mark>

Purpose: Social interaction skills

Equipment: A pair of dice; a table knife and a fork; a hat, scarf, and gloves; a wrapped candy bar

Group Size: For small groups of 6-8 players

Setting: Gym, classroom, or outdoors

DESCRIPTION: This is another fun social interaction game. The groups are seated in a circle in chairs or on the floor. Each group is given a bag containing a pair of gloves (feet ends of nylon hose will work), a hat, a scarf, a table knife and fork, a large chocolate bar which has been securely wrapped (several layers of paper and tied with a ribbon), and a pair of dice.

After a starting signal is given, the players take turns rolling the dice. When two of a kind (doubles) are rolled, that player goes to the center of the circle where other supplies are located and does the following:

1. Puts on all articles of clothing---hat, scarf, gloves.

2. Uses the knife and fork to begin unwrapping the candy bar (dinner). Players do not know contents of the package at this time.

At the same time this is going on, other members of the group continue to take turns rolling the dice. If and when doubles are rolled again, this player will trade places with the person in the center. The clothing articles are exchanged, and the new player continues to open the "dinner"---using the knife and fork. When the "dinner" is eventually unwrapped, the person in the center starts to eat it and shares it with the other players.

Teacher Tips:	• Doubles are often rolled many times during the game, so a lot of playing time is spent dressing and undressing. This may happen so rapidly that the person in the center never gets to the unwrapping of the "surprise package."
	• Players might need to be reminded that they must always use the knife and fork for opening and eating. They should be wearing all articles of clothing before opening or eating.

Shout the Sum

Age Appeal: First Grade and Up

Also good for teens, adults, and seniors

Purpose: Social interaction and basic math skills

Equipment: None

Group Size: Players are with partners

Great for a "Rainy Day"

Setting: Gym, classroom, or outdoors

DESCRIPTION: Divide the students into pairs. Each player stands facing a partner. Each player has both arms behind his back. Both players say, "One, two, three, go." On the word "go" each player extends 0 to 10 fingers so they can be easily seen by the partner.

The object of this game is to be the first player to quickly add up the total of the extended fingers of both players and to shout the sum. For example, if one player has three fingers showing and the other player has all ten fingers showing, then the first player to shout "13" would receive one point. Play continues for 1-2 minutes. At the end of this time period, the students are asked to find a different partner and play again.

Teacher Tips:

- Players will need to be reminded to speak clearly and in unison. "1, 2, 3, ... go!"

- A demonstration of this game really helps the students understand and will make your teaching easier.

- Young children can play with one hand instead of two.

- Try using this game for basic multiplication tables. The players use one hand or two and multiply the number of fingers showing. For example, if one player had five fingers showing and the other player had seven fingers, the answer would be 35.

- Groups of three or four can play by adding the total number of fingers showing. In this version, only one hand of each player is used.

Three Way Keepaway

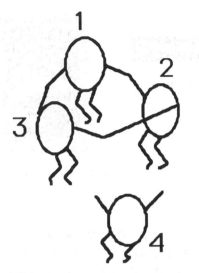 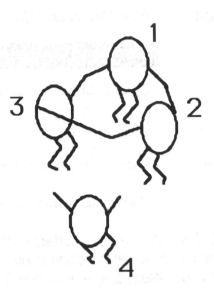

Age Appeal:	Third Grade and Up

Purpose:	Cardiovascular fitness
Equipment:	None
Group Size:	For small groups of 4 players
Setting:	Gym or outdoors

DESCRIPTION: Divide the class into groups of four players. Each participant numbers off 1,2,3 or 4. Players #1, #2 and #3 hold hands to form a small circle. Player #4 stands outside the circle. Player #1 stands directly across from player #4.

On the signal to begin, Player #4 will try to tag player #1. The players in the small circle will rotate to "protect" player #1 from being tagged. Play stops when player #1 is tagged by player #4, or when about 30 seconds has elapsed. When this happens, the players rotate positions. For example, #1 takes the place of #2, #2 becomes #3, #3 becomes #4, and #4 becomes #1. The game continues until all four players have had a chance to be the tagger.

Teacher Tips:	• The tagger cannot reach across or duck under the arms of the players. The tagger has to quickly run to the left or right to tag the runner.
	• Play the game in a round of 30 seconds or less. Fifteen seconds is just fine. This is an extremely physical activity! You will find that the students will get quite a workout.

"56"

Great for a "Rainy Day"

Age Appeal: Third Grade and Up   **Also good for teens, adults, and seniors**

Purpose: Social interaction skills

Equipment: One die for each group

Group Size: For small groups of 5-8 players

Setting: Gym, classroom, or outdoors

DESCRIPTION: The players sit in small circles facing inward. Each group has one die. On a starting signal by the leader, players take turns rolling the die. The object of the game is to be the first group to reach the number 56 (or above). This is done by adding the number of dots showing each time the die is rolled. The first group to finish yells out "56!"

However, any time the number 6 is rolled, it erases the score, and the rolling and adding must begin again. A second and third winner is often appropriate, especially if a team finishes quickly.

Teacher Tips:
- When playing with younger children, you can modify the die so that it only has numbers 1, 2, or 3. This can be done by gluing a piece of paper with "1" on the 4 side, a "2" on the 5 side, and a "sad face" on the 6 side.

- The length of the game is unpredictable. Sometimes it can last 3-4 minutes, other times 1-2 minutes.

Blind Drawing

Great for a "Rainy Day"

Age Appeal: Third Grade and Up ‖ Also good for teens, adults, and seniors

Purpose: Social interaction skills

Equipment: Pencils, paper, and blindfolds (optional)

Group Size: For small groups of 4-6 players

Setting: Gym, classroom, or outdoors

DESCRIPTION: Divide the class into small groups of 4-6 players. Each player is given a sheet of paper and a pencil. Students can also be given a blindfold, or may simply close their eyes. The teacher will direct the students to draw a picture while wearing the blindfold. The teacher gives a step-by-step explanation of what to draw. For example:

Teacher Says:	Students Do:
• "Draw a horse."	Students draw a horse.
• "Put a saddle on the horse."	Students draw a saddle.
• "Place a rider on the saddle."	Students draw a rider.
• "Put a tail on the horse."	Students draw a tail.
• "Draw reins from the mouth of the horse to the hands of the rider."	Students draw the reins.
• "Place a hat on the rider."	Students draw a hat.

After the drawing is finished, the students look at their drawing. Now each student will autograph his drawing. To do this, have the students turn the picture over and place it on the tops of their heads and write their name! Drawings can be posted on a wall for all of the students to view.

Bug Off!

Great for a "Rainy Day"

Age Appeal: Second Grade and Up

Purpose: Social interaction skills

Equipment: Dice, pencils, prepared sheets for each player

Group Size: For small groups of 4 players

Setting: Gym, classroom, or outdoors

DESCRIPTION: This is a fun partner activity, where one set of partners is matched against another. The partners are seated across from each other at a small table (or on the floor). Every player has a pencil and a "Bug Off!" Sheet. Each group of 4 also has one die. The object of the game is to be the first team to draw a picture of a bug. To play, the participants take turns rolling the die. Specific numbers correspond to a body part of a bug. Here is the way the game is played:

If the Number Rolled is...	The Player Draws a(n) ...
1	Body
2	Head
3	Eye
4	Feeler
5	Tail
6	Leg

In order to start drawing, a "1" or a "2" must be rolled first. If a "1" is rolled, then the legs and tail can be added. If a "2" is rolled, then eyes or feelers can be added. Likewise, an eye or a feeler cannot be drawn unless the head was drawn first. The same idea holds for legs and the tail. They cannot be drawn until the body is drawn. Each time a "playable" number is rolled, both the "roller" and his or her partner, draw the designated body part on their sheet. When the person rolling can play (add a body part), he continues to roll until a play can no longer be made. Only one body part can be added at a time. For example, if a "6" is rolled, only one leg can be drawn.

At this point, the die is passed to the next "roller." Play continues until one partnership completes the entire drawing. At this point, the winning couple yells loudly, "Bug off!" and all other players in the room stop playing. Each body part has a specific number, and these are totaled and recorded in the lower portion of the box. Of course, partners will have the same total for that round. At the end of each round, participants will change partners. Partners with the lowest total (for that round) will stay where they are, and partners with the highest score will move to a new table (or spot on the floor). The teacher will determine the rotation procedure and direct the players. Once the players have moved, all of the players have a new partner, and the next round begins.

Bug Off! Sheet

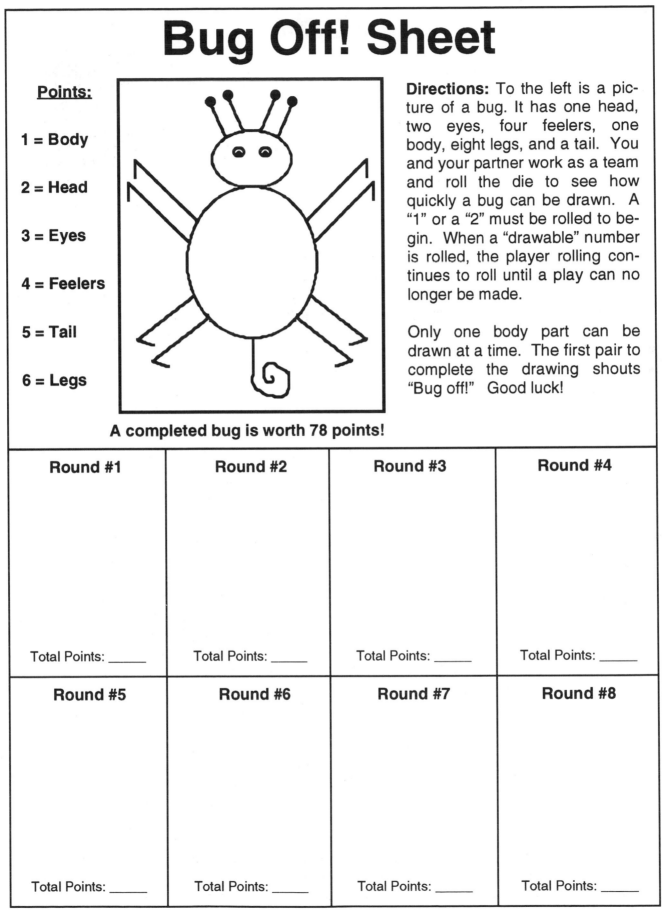

Points:

1 = Body

2 = Head

3 = Eyes

4 = Feelers

5 = Tail

6 = Legs

Directions: To the left is a picture of a bug. It has one head, two eyes, four feelers, one body, eight legs, and a tail. You and your partner work as a team and roll the die to see how quickly a bug can be drawn. A "1" or a "2" must be rolled to begin. When a "drawable" number is rolled, the player rolling continues to roll until a play can no longer be made.

Only one body part can be drawn at a time. The first pair to complete the drawing shouts "Bug off!" Good luck!

A completed bug is worth 78 points!

Round #1	Round #2	Round #3	Round #4
Total Points: _____	Total Points: _____	Total Points: _____	Total Points: _____
Round #5	**Round #6**	**Round #7**	**Round #8**
Total Points: _____	Total Points: _____	Total Points: _____	Total Points: _____

Nature Games

Age Appeal: Third Grade and Up   `Also good for teens, adults, and seniors`

Purpose: Outdoor education and teamwork skills

Equipment: Varies with each activity listed below

Group Size: For small groups of 3-4 players

Setting: Outdoors

Game #1 - LISTEN: This is a fun listening activity. Divide the class into small groups of 3-4 players. Each player is given a 3"x5" card and a pencil and sits in the designated area. The teacher keeps time and for three minutes the players write down all of the sounds they can hear. At the conclusion of the three-minute period, one player reads his list. A point is scored for each sound heard. Other players add to the list of sounds. The cards can be retained and used again at a different time of day or night. A cumulative score can be kept and a winner declared later.

Game #2 - NATURE HUNT: Once again, divide the class into small groups of 3-4 players. A display of 10-15 local items from nature (acorn, feather, maple leaf, small rock, etc.) are viewed by all players for about 3 minutes. They are asked to remember the items, but not to write them down. The display is then removed from sight and the game is ready to begin. The class is given 10-15 minutes to locate and collect as many of the viewed items as possible. When time is called, teams assemble with their collection. The nature display is brought back out and matching items are counted. A point is scored for each duplication and a point is subtracted for each omission. The team with the highest score is declared the winner.

Tired Chief Sitting Bull

Game #3 - SCAVENGER HUNT: Each group receives an envelope with a message like the following inside:

"Our Indian Chief, Sitting Bull, has not slept for 20 nights. We can cure him with our secret sleeping brew, but we need your help. Please bring us the following ingredients 15 minutes from now."

Sample List: 4 dead insects, 20 pine needles, samples of 3 different colors of dirt, 2 red leaves, a shiny stone, small piece of green moss, etc.

The winner would be the group that finds the most items during the playing time.

Game #4 - SQUARE FOOT DIG: Divide the class into groups of 2 or 3 players. Each player has a small garden trowel or other digging implement. One player gets a stick, and tosses it over his back. The spot where the stick lands determines where the group digs. Approximately one square foot of soil comprises the boundaries. After each group has found and marked off their "spot," the teacher gives the signal to start. For 10 minutes, the groups dig up their ground and collect as many different items as possible from their soil. At the end of playing time, items are viewed by others and counted. The group with the most items is determined the winner.

Teacher Tips:
- Groups might need guidance in determining the square foot boundaries.

- Groups may not add items after the ending time is called or items found outside the square foot boundaries.

Game #5 - TREASURE HUNT: Each team of 6-8 players is given a sealed envelope. A leader explains that in the envelope is a clue that will lead the team to a place where a second clue is located. From there, directions will be found that will continue to lead the group, until finally they will find a treasure.

Once the treasure is found, or when they hear a whistle blow (indicating that time is up), the players are to return to the starting place. Groups should not touch clues that might belong to another group. It is best if each group follows a different route for this activity, but if that is not practical or possible, directions for reaching the treasure should vary.

For Example: A card in the envelope might read, "Go to the tallest pine tree you can see from here." The next card might read, "Locate a bush with yellow flowers blooming and go there to find your next clue." A third card might read, "Walk 30 paces towards the creek, find a flat rock and look under it." Approximately 6-10 clues should be used. All groups are winners if they find the treasure. The treasure could be something to eat or keep. Groups should return all clues and envelopes to the leader. This is assurance that no shortcuts were taken in pursuit of the treasure.

Game #6 - QUIZ PROGRAM: Similar to a TV quiz show, nature-oriented questions are prepared in advance that are age and subject appropriate. Participants are divided into groups of 3-4 and answer collectively when it's their turn. Points can be awarded for correct answers, and the group with the most points at the end of playing time is the winner.

Trust Jogging

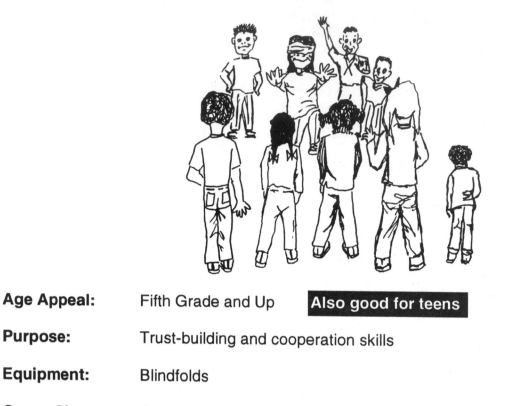

Age Appeal: Fifth Grade and Up   Also good for teens

Purpose: Trust-building and cooperation skills

Equipment: Blindfolds

Group Size: Small group of 7-10 participants

Setting: Gym or outdoors

DESCRIPTION: This trust-building activity is great with a small group of students. Half of the group stand opposite each other about 30-50 feet apart. One player puts on a blindfold. The challenge is to carefully jog to the opposite line of students. The jogger places his hands in front of his body and begins to jog. The jogger is met by members on the other side with outstretched arms. When this happens, the jogger is to slow down. A person on the receiving side then takes a turn by repeating the activity to the opposite side. This continues until every player has had a turn.

Teacher Tips:	• Remind all players to be alert and attentive.
	• If a jogger strays while traveling, players from the opposite line will quickly move to meet the player.
	• Players in the receiving line should not talk. Silence creates more of a trust challenge.
	• For safety reasons, players should always go one at a time.

Cross the Creek

Age Appeal: Kindergarten to Third Grade

Purpose: Jumping skills

Equipment: Two long ropes for each group of 6-8 players

Group Size: Small groups of 6-8 participants

Setting: Gym or outdoors

DESCRIPTION: Divide the class into small groups of 6-8 players. Two long ropes are placed as shown at a distance apart that will be challenging to the children. The space between the ropes is the "creek" and behind each rope is the "bank."

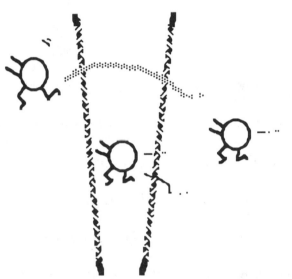

To play, the children jump back and forth from one "bank" to the other, trying not to fall into the "creek." To account for various levels of skill, position ropes so they become further apart (wider creek area) at one end. To make this activity more like a game, you can have the children who miss a jump and land in the "creek" move to a designated area, take their shoes and socks off, immediately put them back on, and return to the game.

Toe Tag

Age Appeal: Third Grade and Up

Purpose: General agility skills

Equipment: None

Group Size: For partners

Setting: Gym or outdoors

DESCRIPTION: Divide the class into partners and have them stand back to back. On a signal to start (given by players to themselves) partners turn around to face each other. The object of this game is for a player to lightly tap the top of the partner's tennis shoe, while preventing a tap on his tennis shoe. The first person to tap a partner three times is the winner. Additional rounds of this game are fun. Partners can play two out of three games to determine a winner. New partnerships can then be formed so winners are paired together.

There is also a version where all of the students form a circle. In this version, all of the players hold hands and face inward in a circle. On the leader's signal to start, the players try to tap the top of the nearest foot of players on both sides while keeping others from tapping their own feet. When both feet of a player have been tapped, he is eliminated. Hands are joined again and play continues. This game is usually short-lived, but very vigorous.

Pop Up

Age Appeal: Third to Sixth Grade

Purpose: Group cooperation skills

Equipment: Blankets and beach balls

Group Size: Small groups of 6-8 participants

Setting: Gym or outdoors

DESCRIPTION: Divide the class into small groups of 6-8 players. Each group is given a blanket. The children stand around the edge of the blanket and hold it with both hands. A beach ball is placed in the middle of the blanket. The object is for the group to work together to pop the ball into the air and catch it again. Challenge each group to:

- See how many times in succession they can toss and catch the ball.
- See if they can continually improve their own number of successful catches.

Shoe Box Rock

Age Appeal: Second to Fifth Grade

Purpose: General coordination skills

Equipment: Plenty of old shoe boxes, rubber bands

Group Size: Small groups of 6-8 participants

Setting: Gym

DESCRIPTION: This activity involves a series of various challenges that can be done with a shoe box. Listed are sample sequences and descriptions. Secure the top of the box with a rubber band and give each student a shoe box. Try these fun progressions:

Throwing and Catching:

- Throw the box as high into the air as possible and catch it.

- Throw the box high into the air, flip it, and catch it.

- Throw and catch with a partner. See how many different ways the box can be thrown. Play a catching game with a rule that you may never throw the box the same way more than once.

Dribbling:

- Place the box on the floor and dribble it around the floor like a soccer ball.

- Dribble the box through a maze or obstacle course.

- With a partner and using one box, play a game of "Keep Away." One partner dribbles the box away. The other partner tries to gain possession, and when successful, dribbles it away.

Box Skating:

- Remove the rubber band and place one foot in each part of the box (top and bottom.) Alone or with a partner, move to the rhythm of popular music.

- When appropriate, give verbal directions to the students: "Take one foot out of the box, turn completely around, and return your foot to the box." "Turn around using the other foot."

115

Touch Ball

Age Appeal: Fourth Grade and Up

Purpose: Throwing, catching, and agility skills

Equipment: Large foam balls

Group Size: For small groups of 5-8 players

Setting: Gym or outdoors

DESCRIPTION: Divide the class into groups of 5-8 players. The players stand in circle formation. One player, IT, stands in the middle of the circle. A ball is passed from player to player across the circle. IT tries to touch the ball and, if successful, trades places with the person who threw that ball.

Teacher Tips:
- Vary the size of the ball--larger is easiest. Use a ball that won't hurt the players--foam or soft rubber.

- Keep the circles small. Increase the difficulty by enlarging the circle.

- Have several players in the center of the circle trying to catch the ball instead of touching it. The game then becomes "Catch Ball."

I Believe in Children

Author Unknown

There is faith in their eyes, love in their touch and hope in their attitude.

I thrill with them at life's joys, run with them through tall grasses and bow with them in worship.

They are the fragile dreams of yesterday, life's radiant reality today and the vibrant stuff of tomorrow.

Yes, I believe in children.

Motivation: The success of a lesson or a planned recreational event depends on the interest of the group and interest-building capacity of the teacher/leader. The teacher must be sold on what he is doing. The teacher should:

- Be enthusiastic about the lesson, games and activities and be able to transfer a feeling of excitement and enthusiasm to the students.

- Know that a friendly welcome makes a positive impression. For example, at a planned recreational-social event, requesting assistance from the first people to arrive gives them something helpful and positive to do.

- Realize that the first game or activity will set the tone for the rest of the class or event.

- Help every member of the group feel a part of and involved with the spirit of the activity. The participants' ability to feel comfortable and fit in will ensure involvement and a positive attitude.

- Give attention to the timing of the activities. A well planned lesson will foster a feeling of ease with the students. Teachers should strive to develop a feeling of genuine fun and accomplishment with the participants.

Personal Thoughts About Awards: We need to give thought to the common practice of rewarding performance with prizes and awards. Awards are often given to recognize specific accomplishments and to motivate others to aspire to do the same. In the realm of games and contests, elaborate awards are not always necessary or appropriate.

Students crave verbal praise and recognition. Prizes and awards often foster an attitude of winning at any cost (bending the rules, cheating, trying to beat the system.) Playing for the sheer sake of fun, enjoyment, personal challenge and team spirit should be emphasized. However, when rewards are expected or thought to be an asset, careful considerations need to be addressed:

- Do awards to a few winners cause many others to feel inadequate or unhappy?

- Are there a variety of awards available for recognition of accomplishments in addition to those given for winning?

- Can winning be defined so that not only the first to finish is recognized? For instance: "Winners" are those who finish within a predetermined time frame. "Winners" are those who did better than they had done previously. "Winners" are those who do their best and don't give up.

5 Great Tag Games:
"Add Sparkle to Your Day!"

Tag games are popular and appealing to a wide range of players. Most tag games are easy to understand, are quickly taught and learned, and provide a lot of action for the youngsters.

Provide for Maximum Participation: However, all components of tag games are not always sound, and some do not provide for maximum participation. Many tag games are constructed so that once a player is "tagged," he is removed from the game. Those who probably need to play the most are usually excluded early in the game.

Rules can be altered to prevent this from happening in some of the following ways:

- Give a specific assignment to the person tagged. For example, taking shoes and socks off, putting them on again, then reentering the game.

- Let those who are tagged help IT tag other players, change teams and continue playing, or help judge or referee the game.

- Limit the length of time for each game. If a game only lasts for two minutes, then the players who are tagged can reenter the next game.

Play It Safe: Since tag games are so physically active, please help keep each game as safe as possible. Use the following suggestions:

- Provide a soft object (foam wand or foam ball) to be held by IT and used for tagging.

- Check out the playing area and surface before playing the tag game. The playing area should be free of holes and sharp objects; boundary lines safely away from walls, bleachers, etc.

- Be sure the participants are appropriately dressed using tennis-type shoes.

- Consider the duration of the playing time and the range of the players' skill/fitness levels.

Point It Out: It is always wise to clearly identify the player who is IT. This can be accomplished by having IT wear a hat or using a soft foam ball to tag players. Try to keep groups small or have more than one IT. Feel free to alter the rules of a tag game if certain players try to get caught so they can be IT. For example, everyone in the group has to be IT before a player can be IT a second time.

Add On Tag

Age Appeal: Third Grade and Up   **Also good for teens and adults**

Purpose: Cardiovascular fitness and social interaction skills

Equipment: None

Group Size: A medium-sized group of 16 to 30 players

Setting: Gym or outdoors

DESCRIPTION: This is a fun partner tag game. All of the players hold hands with a partner. One pair is IT and chases the other pairs. When a pair is caught, they link up with the IT pair by holding hands. The game continues with IT growing bigger and bigger. Each time a couple is tagged, they link up (hold hands). The last couple caught begins the new game as the IT pair.

Teacher Tips:	• Remind the students who are IT to keep their hands connected.
	• Only the two players at either end of IT are able to tag.
	• As IT "grows," you may want to divide IT into two smaller sections. In this way, you'll have more taggers and more excitement!

Crazy Spot Tag

Age Appeal: First Grade and Up   **Also good for teens and adults**

Purpose: Cardiovascular fitness and social interaction skills

Equipment: None

Group Size: A medium-sized group of 16 to 30 players

Setting: Gym or outdoors

DESCRIPTION: One player is selected to be IT. Whenever IT tags a player, that player must hold on to the spot tagged. For example, if IT tags a player on the shoulder, that player must place his hand on his shoulder. This player is not out of the activity, but continues to play while holding his shoulder. If a player is tagged on the knee, that player must put his hand on his knee. If a player is tagged again, that second spot must also be held. If a player is tagged a third time, this player also becomes IT and helps to tag the remaining players.

Handshake Tag

Age Appeal: Kindergarten to Third Grade   **Also good for teens and adults**

Purpose: Cardiovascular fitness and social interaction skills

Equipment: Small foam ball for IT to carry

Group Size: A medium-sized group of 16 to 30 players

Setting: Gym or outdoors

DESCRIPTION: One player is selected to be IT. IT carries a small foam ball for tagging players. The foam ball also helps to let the other players know who is IT. In this tag game, the runners are safe when shaking hands with another person. A handshake can only last 10 seconds, and then runners must break apart to find a new person.

Before each round of the game begins, the teacher announces the number of players the students must shake hands with to be safe. For example, the teacher may say "three." In this case, the students will only be safe if they are shaking hands in groups of three players. If a player is tagged, this player becomes the new IT. The foam ball is given to the new IT as the game continues.

Tunnel Freeze Tag

Age Appeal: Kindergarten and Up

Purpose: Cardiovascular fitness and social interaction skills

Equipment: None

Group Size: A medium-sized group of 16 to 30 players

Setting: Gym or outdoors

DESCRIPTION: One player is selected to be IT. When a runner is tagged, he freezes and stands with his legs spread apart. This player is "frozen" until another active player crawls through the space between the legs. Once a "frozen" player has been set free, he continues to play. If a player is tagged in the process of crawling through, both players are frozen (crawling player stands up nearby). The game is over when all of the players are frozen or when time (usually 3-4 minutes) has been called.

Nose-to-Toes Tag

Age Appeal: Kindergarten and Up   **Also good for teens and adults**

Purpose: Cardiovascular fitness and social interaction skills

Equipment: A small foam ball or other object for IT to carry

Group Size: A medium-sized group of 16 to 30 players

Setting: Gym or outdoors

DESCRIPTION: One player is selected to be IT. In this fun tag game, the students are safe when they hold their nose with one hand and their toes with the other hand. As you can imagine, this has to be done while balancing on one foot. If a player loses balance, he or she can be tagged by IT. If tagged by IT, this player becomes the new IT.

Squat Tag

Age Appeal: Kindergarten and Up

Purpose: Cardiovascular fitness
and social interaction skills

Equipment: A small foam ball or other
object for IT to carry

Group Size: A medium-sized group of 16 to
30 players

Setting: Gym or outdoors

DESCRIPTION: One player is selected to be IT. In this game, the players are safe when squatting with both hands on the floor. However, only 3 "safety squats" are allowed during the game. If tagged by IT, this player becomes the new IT.

Variation: Let the person who is IT decide how many safety squats are allowed per game.

Aerobic Tag

Age Appeal: Third Grade and Up   <mark>Also good for teens and adults</mark>

Purpose: Cardiovascular fitness and social interaction skills

Equipment: Stopwatch, colored vests, ball or frisbee

Group Size: Any size

Setting: Gym or outdoors

DESCRIPTION: The participants are divided into two teams. Each team is identified by wearing colored vests. The purpose of the game is for a team to retain possession of an "object" (ball or frisbee) for a predetermined number of seconds (contingent upon age of players and size of playing area.)

To begin, the "object" is thrown randomly into the air by the leader. Any player may grab it and attempt to keep it away from the opposing team. If the player in possession of the "object" is tagged (both hands above the waist) by a member of the opposing team, the tagging team gains possession, the time on the stopwatch is cleared, and play resumes. When the "object" switches from one team to the other, the leader calls out "Change" and simultaneously stops the watch and starts it again. When one team keeps possession of the "object" for 30 seconds, the leader calls out "Time" and the winning team is recognized.

Teacher Tip:	• If played outside, a definite playing area should be determined. An area about the size of a gym is appropriate for young players. Big groups and/or older players would be better challenged on a football/soccer type field.

The Cat and the Rats

Age Appeal:	Kindergarden to Third Grade **Also good for teens and adults**
Purpose:	Cardiovascular fitness and social interaction skills
Equipment:	None
Group Size:	A medium-sized group of 16 to 30 players
Setting:	Gym or outdoors

DESCRIPTION: The players hold hands in a circle facing inward. One "cat" is selected and stands on the outside of the circle. One or several "rats" are appointed and stand inside the circle. To begin, the following conversation occurs between the cat and rats:

Cat: "I am the cat."	**Rats:** "We are the rats."
Cat: "I can catch you!"	**Rats:** "No! You can't!"

The cat then chases the rats and tries to tag them. The players in the circle try to protect the rats by keeping the cat out when the rats are in and the cat in when the rats are out. When a rat is caught, it retires to the circle. If the cat gets tired or is unsuccessful in catching any rats after a minute or two, he can tag a player in the circle (who has not been a cat or rat in the game) who becomes the cat. The last rat to be tagged is the winner and gets to choose a new cat for the next game.

Charlie Over the Water

Age Appeal: Kindergarden to Third Grade

Purpose: Cardiovascular fitness and social interaction skills

Equipment: None

Group Size: A medium-sized group of 16 to 30 players

Setting: Gym or outdoors

DESCRIPTION: The children stand facing inward and holding hands in a circle. One (or more) players are selected to be "Charlie" and stand in the center. Children in the circle walk (skip, gallop, jog) around as they chant:

> "Charlie over the water,
> Charlie over the sea,
> Charlie caught a blackbird
> But he can't catch me."

On the word, "me," the children in the circle quickly squat and place both hands on the floor in front of them before Charlie can tag them. If tagged, that player trades places with Charlie and the game continues.

Teacher Tips:	•	The size of the circle must be realistic for Charlie to have a chance for tagging.
	•	Vary the pose that players perform in order to be safe (sitting cross-legged on the floor--standing on one foot with hands clasped above head, etc.)

Cranes and Crows

–"Cranes!"

Crows		Cranes

Safety Line — Safety Line

Age Appeal: Kindergarden to Third Grade **Also good for teens and adults**

Purpose: Cardiovascular fitness and agility skills

Equipment: None

Group Size: A medium-sized group of 16 to 30 players

Setting: Gym or outdoors

DESCRIPTION: A playing area about the size of a basketball court is marked off with side boundary lines and back safety lines. Restraining lines are marked three feet back on either side from center line, and run the width of the court. Players are divided into two teams-- the Crows and the Cranes. Each team lines up facing each other across a six-foot neutral area.

To play, the teacher calls out either "Crows" or "Cranes." The players on the team called must try to run back and cross their safety line (behind them) without being tagged by players on the opposite team. Players never know which team will be called, so they must stay ready to either run or chase. When a player is caught, he changes over to the other team. Players return to their restraining lines after each chase, and play begins again. A game is won when all players from one team are caught and everyone is on the same side.

Teacher Tip:	• The leader can add fun and suspense to the game by drawing out the call--- "Crrrrrr---".

126

Lame Fox

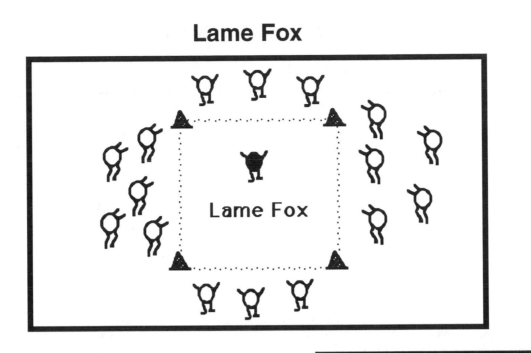

Age Appeal: Kindergarden to Third Grade   **Also good for teens and adults**

Purpose: Agility and social interaction skills

Equipment: Cones to mark off the Fox's den

Group Size: A medium-sized group of 16 to 30 players

Setting: Gym or outdoors

DESCRIPTION: One player (or more if the group is large) is chosen to be the "Fox." He starts the game by standing in his den, which is the middle one-third of the playing area and marked accordingly. To play, the fox is teased by other players who call out...

"Lame fox! Lame fox! Can't catch anybody!"

as they run back and forth across his den. The object of the game is for the fox to catch other players. The fox can do this in several ways:

- He can run and tag them as they cross his den,

- He may take 3 steps outside of his den as he tries to catch them,

- He may hop <u>anywhere</u> in the play area in order to catch them.

If he takes more than 3 steps outside of his den or forgets to hop when he should, he must return to his den and anyone tagged during that time is not caught. If the fox is successful and does catch someone, that person takes his place as the fox and the game continues.

Octopus Tag

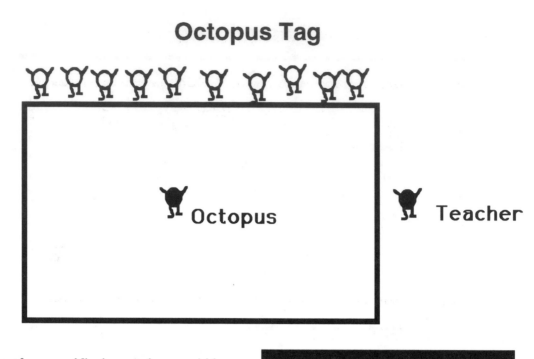

Age Appeal:	Kindergarden and Up	**Also good for teens and adults**
Purpose:	Cardiovascular fitness and social interaction skills	
Equipment:	None	
Group Size:	A medium-sized group of 16 to 30 players	
Setting:	Gym or outdoors	

DESCRIPTION: One player is selected to be the "Octopus" (IT) and stands in the middle of the playing area. All other players are "Fish." The teacher calls out, "Cross the ocean." At that time, all of the Fish must "swim" (run) across to the other side of the playing area, while the Octopus tries to tag them. If a Fish reaches the other side without being tagged, the Fish is safe. All of the Fish wait on the other side for the teacher to call out "Cross the ocean" again. When a Fish is tagged, it stays on that spot in the ocean, and turns into a "Tentacle." A Tentacle can sit or stand in one of three ways:

- Standing with feet crossed,   • Seated with legs crossed, or   • Kneeling.

From one of these stationary positions, the Tentacles can reach out and tag the Fish that are crossing the ocean. If tagged by a Tentacle, the Fish is caught and turns into a Tentacle too!

Teacher Tips:	• The game (or round) is over when all the Fish have been caught---usually about 3 minutes.
	• Throughout the game, the leader calls out "Cross The Ocean" before each run. Players must immediately run.

Posture Tag

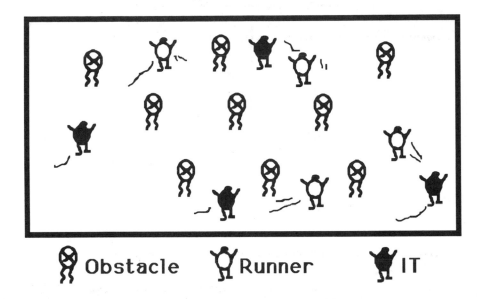

Obstacle   Runner   IT

Age Appeal: Second Grade and Up   **Also good for teens and adults**

Purpose: Cardiovascular fitness and social interaction skills

Equipment: Bean bags

Group Size: A medium-sized group of 16 to 30 players

Setting: Gym or outdoors

DESCRIPTION: The players are divided into 3 groups:

- Obstacles - stand in playing area

- Runners - players being chased

- Chasers - players who are IT

The Runners and Chasers must travel with bean bags on their heads. If a Runner is tagged, he places the bean bag on the head of an "Obstacle" and takes that person's place. A Runner who gets tired may exchange places with an "Obstacle" by placing the bean bag on the head of the "Obstacle" player at any time during the game.

If a bean bag falls off a player, it must be replaced before play can continue. Bean bags may not be held. The game continues until time is called.

Streets and Alleys Tag

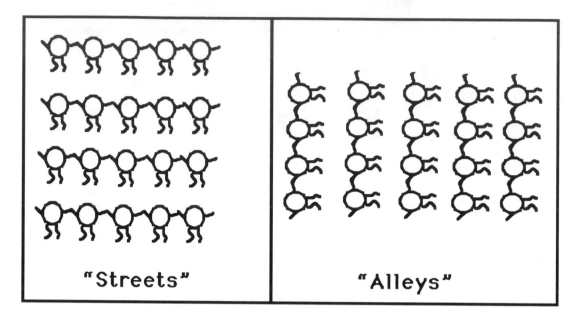

"Streets"   "Alleys"

Age Appeal: Kindergarten and Up   **Also good for teens and adults**

Purpose: Group cooperation skills

Equipment: None

Group Size: A medium-sized group of 16 to 30 players

Setting: Gym or outdoors

DESCRIPTION: The players are organized into lines. When the players join hands and face the front of the playing area, the aisles they make are called "streets," and when they turn and face the side of the playing area and hold hands, the aisles they make are called "alleys."

There are two extra players, a runner and a chaser. They can run only through the aisles made by the other players. These aisles are changed when the teacher calls "Streets" (all join hands facing front) or "Alleys" (all join hands facing side). This quick changing from Streets to Alleys can either help or hinder the chaser. When the runner is caught, both the runner and chaser choose players to take their places, and play begins again.

Walk Tag

Age Appeal: Kindergarten and Up   **Also good for teens and adults**

Purpose: Agility skills

Equipment: None   **Group Size:** Any size

Setting: Gym or outdoors

DESCRIPTION: In this game, the participants choose partners. One partner is the "Walker" and the other is the "Chaser." The object of the game is for the Chaser to tag the Walker. All players must walk during the entire game. To start the game, the teacher counts to "10." This gives the Walker a chance to move away from the Chaser. When "10" is reached all of the Chasers walk as fast as they can and attempt to tag their partner. Any time a Chaser tags his Walker, roles are switched. The new Chaser must count to "10" before starting. In this game the play is continuous.

Variation: A fun variation of this game consists of making the playing area increasingly smaller. This can be done by using a rope that is as long as the width of the playing area. For example, the rope is held by the teacher and another student at one end of the gym. As the game continues, the teacher and student slowly move the rope so that the playing area becomes smaller and smaller. Players cannot move past the rope boundary. This increases the excitement since the players are now moving in a more restricted area.

Spider Web Tag

Age Appeal: Kindergarten and Up   **Also good for teens and adults**

Purpose: Agility skills

Equipment: Small foam ball for IT   **Group Size:** 16 -30 players

Setting: Gym or outdoors

DESCRIPTION: In this game one player is selected to be the "Spider." The rest of the class scatter in the designated playing area. The Spider will tag the other players ("Flies") with the foam ball. When tagged, the Flies turn into "Webs" and assist the Spider in catching others by holding them until the Spider can tag them with the foam ball.

Flies can wiggle away from a Web and avoid being caught. Only one player can hold a person for the Spider - no "ganging up." The game is over when the last player is caught. That person can either be the new Spider or choose the new Spider.

Slip Away Tag

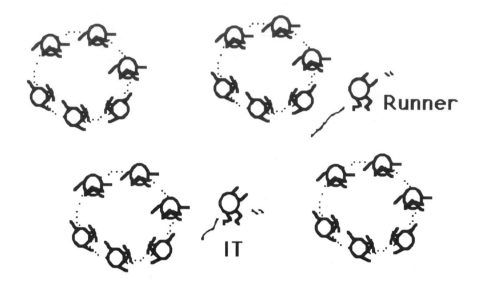

Age Appeal: Second Grade and Up   **Also good for teens**

Purpose: Cooperation and social interaction skills

Equipment: Beanbags

Group Size: A medium-sized group of 16 to 30 players

Setting: Gym or outdoors

DESCRIPTION: Select one player to be "IT" and another player to be the "Runner." The rest of the class is divided into groups of five or six players. Each group sits cross-legged on the ground in circles, facing inward, and scattered throughout the playing area. Each group has a beanbag. Both IT and the Runner have a beanbag too.

On a signal to begin, the players seated in the circles begin to pass the beanbag from one to the other around the circle. The beanbag should travel in the same direction and must be accepted when passed. At the same time, IT tries to tag the Runner.

The Runner is safe when getting into the inside of any circle. When the Runner enters a circle, the seated person who is holding the beanbag at that moment, becomes the new Runner. The original Runner takes the vacated spot in the circle and begins passing the beanbag he is carrying. If IT gets tired or cannot successfully tag the Runner within two minutes, he steps into a circle. The person holding the beanbag then trades places and becomes the new IT. If IT is successful in catching the Runner, the beanbags are exchanged, roles are reversed and the game continues.

Sword Tag

Age Appeal: Third Grade and Up `Also good for teens`

Purpose: Agility and social interaction skills

Equipment: Boffers (or rolled newspaper) and poly spots

Group Size: Small groups of 8-10 players

Setting: Gym or outdoors

DESCRIPTION: Divide the class into small groups of 8-10 players. A boffer (or newspaper rolled up to resemble a sword) is placed on a small circle in the center of the playing area. A frisbee or a poly spot can be used to mark the center. All players stand in a circle about 6-10 feet back from the center. The size of the circle will vary with the age and skills of the players.

One player, IT, stands in the center of the circle. On a signal to start, IT picks up the sword and tags a player in the circle. After a tag, IT quickly takes the sword back and lays (not throws) it in the center, and hurries to take the place in the circle vacated by the person tagged. The "tagged" person hurries to the center, picks up the sword and tries to tag IT before IT can reach the vacated spot.

If tagged, IT must immediately return to the center again, pick up the sword and try to tag the "tagged" person again. The process continues until one player is successful in returning to the vacated spot untagged. When this happens, the game begins again with the unsuccessful player becoming the new IT.

Squirrels and the Fox

Age Appeal: Kindergarten to Fourth Grade

Purpose: Cardiovascular fitness and social interaction skills

Equipment: None

Group Size: Any size

Setting: Gym or outdoors

DESCRIPTION: This game is similar in formation to "Squirrels in the Trees." Players are divided into groups of 3 and each player is given a number --1, 2, or 3. Players 1 and 2 face each other and hold hands to make a "tree". Player 3 is the "squirrel" and stands "in the tree." When the leader/teacher calls out, "Squirrels Run!" the squirrels must leave their "tree" and find another tree. "Trees" should be as widely spaced about the playing area as possible. After squirrels are safely settled in a new "tree" the leader again calls "Squirrels Run!" and play continues as before.

However, in this game there are at least one extra squirrel and a fox. The fox chases the squirrel that is not in a tree. The squirrel is safe when he enters a tree. The squirrel in the tree entered becomes the runner and must leave immediately. If the fox catches a "loose" squirrel, he is a winner and gets to choose a new fox (from a player who is presently a "tree"), and the game begins again.

If the fox is unsuccessful in catching a squirrel after a minute or two, the teacher chooses a new fox from among the "trees." The fox can only tag a squirrel outside of a tree.

Being a Teacher

By Lee Iacocca

In a completely rational society, only the best of us would aspire to be teachers. The rest of us would have to settle for something less. Because the act of passing civilization along from one generation to the next ought to be the highest honor and the biggest responsibility anyone could have.

Get a Jump Start: Good teachers and youth leaders understand the value of having things planned and ready to go at the beginning of each class. There is an obvious "transition time" for elementary-aged students (teenagers and adults as well!) as they move from a small classroom setting to a more open environment such as a large gym or outdoors. Using a variety of Warm-Up Stations is a good way to do this!

1. **Warm-Up Stations-:** As the students come into the gym, they all gather together at a designated location. Around the gym are a variety of Skill-Learning Stations. Each station has enough equipment for 4-5 players. On your directions, the students are free to go to any station and can move to another station if there is space. The use of music enhances this activity.

   Examples of stations may include:

Jump for Joy Station	Individual short jump ropes
Scoop It Up Station	Scoops and balls
Strength Station	Gym mats for doing curl-ups and push-ups
Ball Bonanza Station	Different type balls for catching and throwing
Scooter Town	Obstacle course using scooter boards
Juggle Time Station	Juggling scarves to practice juggling

Teacher Tips:

- Post instructions (on wall or on floor in center of play area) for "challenge practice" on skills previously taught.

- Sound a signal 30-60 seconds before stopping time to allow participants to finish, return equipment and gather together.

- Be conscious of time - allotment for this "pre-class" activity will vary according to the length of the class. For a 40-60 minute class, 10 minutes is sufficient. For classes of less than 40 minutes, 5 minutes is suggested.

- Follow this format on a regular basis. Soon your students will learn to automatically begin when they enter the teaching area. They should never stand around and wait.

Explosive Games and Relays

This chapter contains a great collection of fun relays and games. When dividing the class into relay teams, the leader/teacher should creatively incorporate the process into play. Care should be given to assure fairness, diplomacy, and efficiency. Here are a few suggestions:

Quick and East Ways to Designate Teams: Spend as little time as possible dividing players into groups. Here are a few examples:

- Arm Crossing: The leader asks all participants to cross their arms. All who have the right arm on top become a group and all with the left arm on top form a second group. If one group is larger, ask people in that group to fold their hands together. Those with left thumb on top are then separated from those with right thumb on top. These extra players can be used to balance the teams.

- Bandanna or Color Strips: A collection of laminated strips of colored cardboard or bandannas of different colors are a wise part of a leader/teacher supply inventory. When participants enter the playing area, either the bandanna or colored cardboard can be handed out. When it is time for team division, the students group together by color. The ideal reason for using these items is that they can be collected and reused. A quick activity to use before team division is to ask participants to exchange their color with another person (or two or three) before finally forming teams. Doing this will control team "stacking."

- Birth Months: Depending on how many groups are needed, participants are asked to group together according to the month they were born. For example, if four groups are needed, then use the months January-March, April-June, July-September, and October-December. If groups are uneven after this division, leader directs the changes to even things up.

- "Hand Carving": The leader divides the group into sections (groups) by stretching his or her hands and arms apart and forward to include a desired number of players. This method is effective when exact numbers are not important.

- Partners: The leader instructs all participants to quickly stand back to back with another person. Certain characteristics can be requested, either for the requirements of a forthcoming activity or just for fun (for example, persons who are same size or gender). After this is done, one of the partners goes to one team, and the other partner moves to the second team.

Balloon Frantic

Age Appeal: Third Grade and Up   **Also good for teens and adults**

Purpose: Cooperation and teamwork skills

Equipment: Stopwatch and balloons

Group Size: A medium-sized group of 16 to 30 players

Setting: Gym or outdoors

DESCRIPTION: Before play begins, each participant should have one inflated balloon that is large enough to easily keep batted into the air. On a signal to start, all players hit their balloons upward and do not catch them again during play.

Every 10 seconds, another inflated balloon is put into play by the leader. The object of the game is for the group, working together, to see how long they can keep all of the balloons aloft. A leader keeps time. Several spotters watch for balloons that drop to the ground. If players can retrieve one and get it back into play before it is seen by a spotter, that is good.

The spotter yells loudly (or sounds some type of signal) when a balloon is spotted on the floor. After 6 yells, the round is over and time is noted. Several rounds should be played with improvement in the length of playing time as a group goal.

The Clock

Age Appeal: Third Grade and Up   **Also good for teens and adults**

Purpose: Cooperation and teamwork skills

Equipment: Stopwatch and poly spots

Group Size: A medium-sized group of 16 to 30 players

Setting: Gym or outdoors

DESCRIPTION: The participants sit cross-legged in a circle on the ground, holding hands with people on both sides. On a starting signal, the group stands, circles 360 degrees clockwise, reverses direction and circles 360 degrees back to starting position, and returns to sitting position in as short a time as possible.

All hands must stay clasped for the entire time. If hands break apart, the round should be started again. The object of the activity is for the group, working together, to com-

plete the task in as short a time as possible. A leader keeps track of time with a stop watch. Several rounds should be played, and the group encouraged by the leader to better their time each round. One second for each participant is a challenging goal. For example, if the group has 30 players, then the challenge would be to complete the task within 30 seconds.

Teacher Tips:	• Participants should be reminded to start and finish by sitting on the ground with legs crossed in front.
	• After each round, invite participants to talk and plan for a more successful attempt. Usually, players improve with strategy and experience.

End Ball

Age Appeal: Fourth Grade and Up   **Also good for teens**

Purpose: Catching and throwing skills

Equipment: Two to three large foam balls

Group Size: A medium-sized group of 16 to 30 players

Setting: Gym or outdoors

DESCRIPTION: The players are divided into two teams. Four players on each team are called "Ends" and the rest of the players are the "Guards." A playing area about the size and shape of a basketball court is used. The object of the game is to successfully throw a ball over the heads of opposing Guards so that the ball is caught by a team member standing in the end area.

The game is started with a tip-off between opposing Guards in the center. One point is scored for each successful throw from a Guard to an End of the same team. After a score, the ball stays in play until the end of a quarter. Each quarter lasts five minutes. An End who catches a ball continues play by tossing the ball back to his Guards.

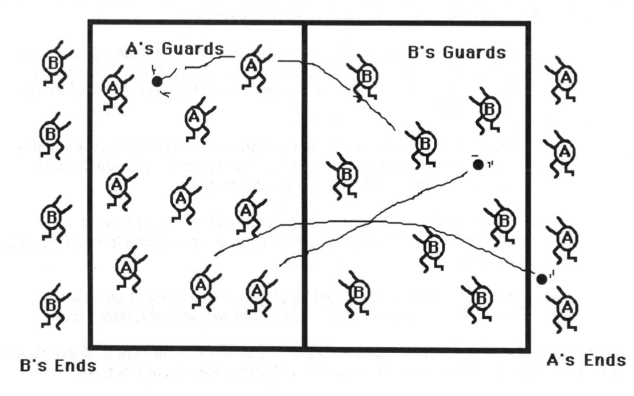

A ball that goes out of the play area is retrieved and put in play from where it went out by any nearby player. A player that steps out of his area loses the ball to the nearest opposing player. A player may not travel with the ball. At the end of every quarter, the players rotate positions so that new players have a chance to be the Ends. Using 12-16 players on a team makes it a very competitive game.

Tennis Ball Frantic

Age Appeal: Fourth Grade and Up   **Also good for teens**

Purpose: Teamwork and basic soccer skills

Equipment: Stopwatch and lots of old tennis balls

Group Size: A medium-sized group of 16 to 30 players

Setting: Gym

DESCRIPTION: This is a fun and challenging game with plenty of physical activity. The game and its just-for-fun vocabulary was developed by Project Adventure. Each participant is given a tennis ball and places it in a pile in the center of the floor. The object of the game is for the players to keep all of the balls moving by kicking or dribbling them with their feet, for as long as possible. The game begins with the teacher kicking the pile of tennis balls so that the balls roll in all directions. Other rules:

- Four students are selected as the "Spotters." The Spotters are spaced around the playing area and watch for stationary balls. When one is found, they yell "Frantic!" This alerts the other players to look for non-moving balls.

- After 4 non-moving balls have been spotted, the round is over and the length of time played is announced by the teacher who has the stopwatch. This time becomes the group's record.

- To add a bit of excitement, the teacher adds a new ball every 10 seconds or so. This makes it more difficult for the class to keep the balls moving!

- More than one round should be played, with the object being for the group to improve the length of time they can keep the balls moving.

To start a new round, all balls must be collected and piled in the center of the playing area. Participants might want a few minutes for strategy planning at this point.

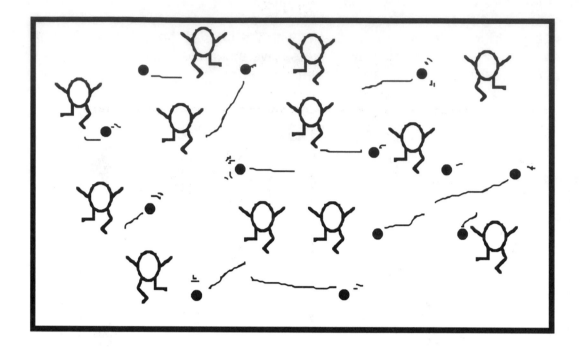

Teacher Tips:	•	This activity is very aerobic. Participants will improve with practice.
	•	Approximately 20 more tennis balls than players will be needed.
	•	This is usually a noisy game; a whistle is helpful with large classes.

Guts

RESTRAINING LINES

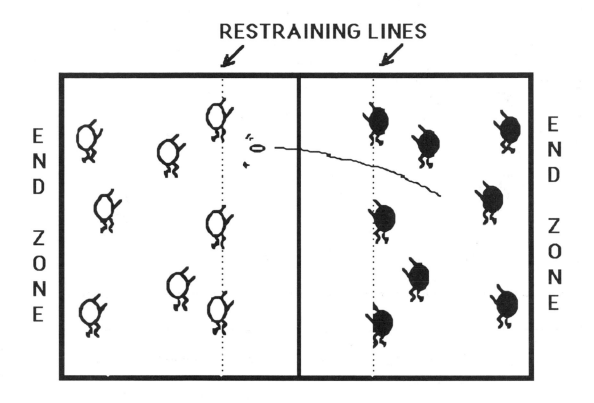

Age Appeal: Third Grade and Up   **Also good for teens and adults**

Purpose: Frisbee catching and throwing skills

Equipment: Several frisbees

Group Size: Any size

Setting: Gym or outdoors

DESCRIPTION: Throwing and catching a frisbee provides much-needed physical activity opportunities for children. Once some degree of skill has been accomplished, games using frisbees can provide fitness, physical movement, and fun. In this game, the players are divided into two teams. A team stands in half of the playing area. An average playing area is approximately the size of a basketball court. However, the size of the playing area will vary according to the skill and number of participants. Players with higher skill levels will generally require a larger playing area.

The object of the game is for a team to successfully throw the frisbee from behind their team's restraining line into the end zone area that is behind their opponents. When this is done, one point is scored. To prevent their opponents scoring, the receiving team can either catch or "bat down" the oncoming frisbee. A frisbee caught inside the end zone does not score. A frisbee that is "batted down" in this area will score if it lands inside the end zone area.

Players may stand anywhere in their territory, including in front of the restraining line or in the end zone area.   Once the frisbee is received, it is thrown back to the opponents court. However, the frisbee must be thrown from behind the restraining line.

Other Rules:

- Players may not travel when in possession of the frisbee.

- If a player is too far back to throw the frisbee to the end zone, the frisbee can be passed to a teammate standing closer to the restraining line.

- Play is continuous until one team has scored a predetermined number of points (10-12) or until time is called (10-15 minutes.)

- If playing in a gym, the wall behind the basketball court can be considered inbounds. In this case, a thrown frisbee that hits the wall and falls to the floor would score one point.

- If appropriate, more than one frisbee can be used to play this game.

Ultimate Frisbee

Age Appeal: Third Grade and Up   **Also good for teens and adults**

Purpose: Cardiovascular fitness and general frisbee skills

Equipment: A frisbee, colored vests to identify teams

Group Size: Any size

Setting: Gym or outdoors

DESCRIPTION: A large, rectangular playing area is used for this game. A football or soccer field is ideal. The players are divided into two teams. Play begins with each team lined up on their own goal line at the ends of the playing field. One team is awarded the frisbee and a starting signal begins play.

The object of the game is for a team to advance the frisbee down the field by throwing

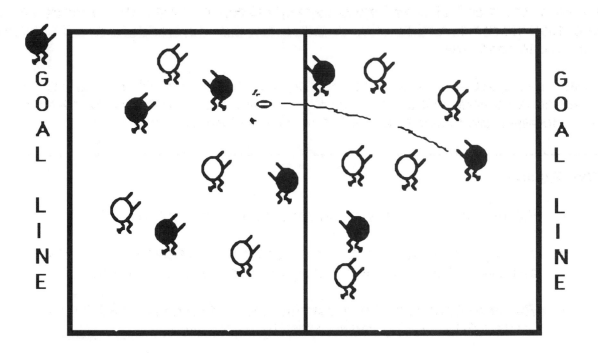

it to teammates. A goal is scored when the frisbee is caught by a player behind the opponent's goal line.

Other Rules:
- Players may not travel with the frisbee. If so, opponents gain possession of the frisbee at the site of the infraction. Play continues from where a foul is committed.

- Any time the frisbee hits the ground, the opposing team gains possession.

- There can be no physical contact. If there is, the opposing team gains possession, or a nonguarded free throw is awarded.

- When a point is scored, players line up on their own goal line again. The nonscoring team gets possession and play begins again.

- A game is won by scoring the most points by the end of the game. Playing time ranges from 15 minutes to an hour, depending on the endurance of the players and available time.

Teacher Tip: Encourage the players to guard and intercept the frisbee, as this is the primary way to gain possession of the frisbee.

No Balls Wanted!

Age Appeal:	Third Grade and Up

Also good for teens

Purpose: Throwing skills

Equipment: Small foam balls, yarn balls, and other soft balls

Group Size: Any size

Setting: Gym

DESCRIPTION: For this game, the players are divided into two teams. Each player has a small ball (foam ball or yarn ball) that is soft and throwable. Each team stands in half of the playing area, which is divided by a center line. On a signal to begin, the players throw the balls into the opponent's area. When the balls are thrown into a team's area, they are quickly returned to the opponent's court.

The object of the game is to have fewer balls in your team's area than your opponent's when the game ends. At the end of the round, the balls are counted and a point given to the team with the fewest balls. Several rounds should be played. Each game can last 2-3 minutes.

Teacher Tips:	• If any balls are thrown after the ending signal is sounded, two balls should be added to the score of the team responsible for the late throw.
	• A neutral area between teams, which increases the throwing distance, adds more challenge to this game.

Four-Way Volleyball

Age Appeal: Fourth Grade and Up   **Also good for teens and adults**

Purpose: Basic volleyball skills

Equipment: Volleyball standards, two long ropes or lengths of plastic flag line, several beach balls

Group Size: Any size

Setting: Gym

DESCRIPTION: Two long ropes or lengths of decorative plastic flag line are strung across the playing area so that they intersect in the middle. Players are divided into 4 teams and each team stands in a quarter of the court. Natural boundaries for each team are imaginary lines directly under the suspended ropes and as far back as the playing area allows. The object is for players to prevent a beach ball from landing in their territory by successfully volleying an oncoming ball to another section of the court. If a ball lands on the floor or is not correctly returned, a point is given to that team.

To play, a leader throws a beach ball into the playing area in any direction. A team can volley the ball any number of times before hitting it over the net to another team, but a person can only volley once. After one ball has been in play for a few minutes, other balls can be added. At the end of the playing time, the team with the fewest number of points is the winner.

Teacher Tips:

- If keeping accurate score is an appropriate factor, a nonplaying score keeper for each team is helpful. It is hard to play and keep up with misses.

- This game is great to use when a group is gathering and "straggling" into the play area. As people arrive, they can be assigned to a team.

- To play with young children, lower the net and allow the students to throw and catch, rather than volley.

Discipline Tip #7: Time It Right

How Many? How Much? How Long? One of the factors to consider when planning a lesson or special event is making sure the lessons and/or games are of the right length or duration. Playing a game for too long will cause the class to lose interest and may cause potential student misbehavior. Also the setting, age of participants, and purpose of the game or activity must be considered. Listed are some "guesstimates" and other suggestions for consideration:

- If directions are being explained, 1-2 minutes should be the limit.
- If an activity is being demonstrated, one minute is long enough.
- An hour and a half is long enough for most social events.
- If a game calls for collecting or listing things, 8-10 minutes are enough.
- If a game consists of rounds, 3-4 minutes are enough for each round.
- Leaders/teachers should always have more games and activities planned than will probably be used. Experience will help a teacher learn to know what to add or cut out and when to do it.
- When planning a recreational social event, a "Family Fun Night" for example, always use your opening and closing activities as planned. If there is a need to adjust, other activities can be deleted, curtailed, or added.
- If a story is being told, 5 minutes is ideal.
- A game or activity that is not going well should be terminated as soon as possible. This can be noted by the actions of the participants. They might be off-task or appear uninterested. A good teacher/leader should continually be alert and sensitive to this.

Balloon-Paddle Relay

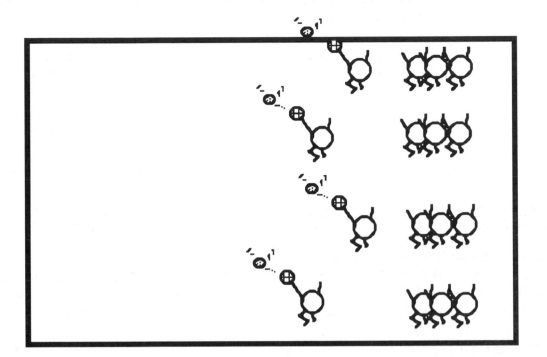

Age Appeal: Third Grade and Up   <mark>Also good for teens and adults</mark>

Purpose: Teamwork and eye-hand coordination skills

Equipment: Balloons and racquets

Group Size: Any size

Setting: Gym or outdoors

DESCRIPTION: Divide the class into groups of 3-4 players.

Teacher Tip: It is always better to have small teams when doing relays. This is good for several reasons - it allows more students to be physically active, there is less off-task time and more time to practice the skill, and there will be fewer student behavioral problems.

Every team is given an inflated balloon and a paddle or tennis racquet. On a signal to start, the team members take turns batting the balloon in the air with the paddle to a designated turning line and back. Challenge the class to see how many times they can complete the relay in a 2-3 minute time period.

Blackboard Relay

Age Appeal: Third Grade and Up

Purpose: General academic content knowledge

Equipment: Blackboard and chalk

Group Size: Any size

Setting: Classroom or gym

Great for a "Rainy Day"

DESCRIPTION: Divide the class into groups of 3-4 players. The teams are positioned so they are the same distance from a blackboard. The first player in each team has a piece of chalk. The teacher announces a spelling word or an appropriate question. Each of the groups has about 30 seocnds to confer on the answer.

On the signal to start, the first player in line quickly walks to the blackboard and writes the first letter of the word or answer. When the player finishes writing the letter, he quickly walks back and hands the piece of chalk to the next player. This continues until the answer is written on the chalkbard. For example:

Teacher:	The Students Would Write:
"What is the capitol of North Carolina?"	R-a-l-e-i-g-h
"What number do you dial in an emergency?	9-1-1
"Which planet is closest to the sun?"	M-e-r-c-u-r-y
"What is the name of the fastest land animal?"	C-h-e-e-t-a-h

Command Relay

Age Appeal: Kindergarten and Up   **Also good for teens and adults**

Purpose: Cooperation and teamwork skills

Equipment: None

Group Size: Any size

Setting: Outdoors

DESCRIPTION: Divide the class into groups of 3-4 players. The teacher describes a characteristic of objects within the playing area. For example: "Touch something hard." The first students in line look around the playing area for an object that matches that description, run and touch it, and run back to tag the next player in line. The next player will run and tag the same object, or another object matching the same characteristic. Players tag teammates, one after another, until each player has had a turn. The round is over when all players have finished.

Sample statements:
- "Touch something flat."
- "Touch something red."
- "Touch something made of metal."
- "Touch something taller than yourself."

Link Relay

Age Appeal: Kindergarten and Up   **Also good for teens and adults**

Purpose: Cooperation and teamwork skills

Equipment: None

Group Size: Any size

Setting: Gym or outdoors

DESCRIPTION: Divide the class into groups of 6-8 players. Team members link up as partners and travel in a predetermined manner as they complete the relay. For example, if the teacher says:

Teacher Command:	Students Will:
"Elbow to elbow"	Link elbows together and run
"Hands to hip"	Place a hand on the partner's hip and quickly walk
"Back-to-back"	Walk back-to-back to do the relay

Hula Hoop Relay

Age Appeal: Second Grade and Up   **Also good for teens**

Purpose: Cooperation and teamwork skills

Equipment: Hula hoops

Group Size: Any size

Setting: Gym or outdoors

DESCRIPTION: Divide the class into groups of 3-4 players. Team members run to a designated turning line where a hula hoop is placed. Each member will hold the hoop like a jump rope and jump it three times as they recite the first verse of a predetermined nursey rhyme or chant. The relay continues until the entire rhyme is finished. The rhyme or chant should be practiced by all of the students prior to the relay. For example:

Runner:	Will Say:
#1	"Twinkle, twinkle, little star..."
#2	"How I wonder what you are."
#3	"Up above the world so high..."
#4	"Like a diamond in the sky."

Posture Relay

Age Appeal: Second Grade and Up

Also good for teens and adults

Purpose: Cooperation and teamwork skills

Equipment: Beanbags

Group Size: Any size

Setting: Gym or outdoors

DESCRIPTION: Divide the class into groups of 3-4 players. Team members run to a designated turning line and back while balancing a beanbag on their head. If the beanbag falls off, the student must stop and put it back on his or her head.

Teacher Tip: It is also possible to balance the beanbag on other parts of the body, like shoulders, elbows, back of the hand, etc.

Rescue Relay

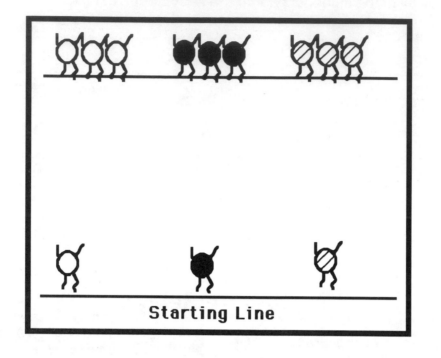

Starting Line

Age Appeal: Kindergarten and Up   **Also good for teens and adults**

Purpose: Cardiovascular fitness and teamwork skills

Equipment: None

Group Size: Any size

Setting: Gym or outdoors

DESCRIPTION: Divide the class into groups of 3-4 players. The first player stands at the starting line. The rest of the team players stand on another line opposite the first player. On a signal to begin, the first player runs across and takes one teammate by the hand and the two of them return to the starting line. The first runner stays at the starting line as the second runner crosses over and takes another teammate by the hand. The relay continues until all of the players are on the starting line.

Variation: Here is another fun modification to this relay. The first player runs across and takes a teammate by the hand and goes back to the starting line. After crossing the starting line, both players run back, get the third player and return to the starting line. Now all three players run and get the last player. In this way, the relay begins with one player and ends with all four players crossing the starting line! The first runner gets the best workout and the last player gets the least.

Hoopla Relay

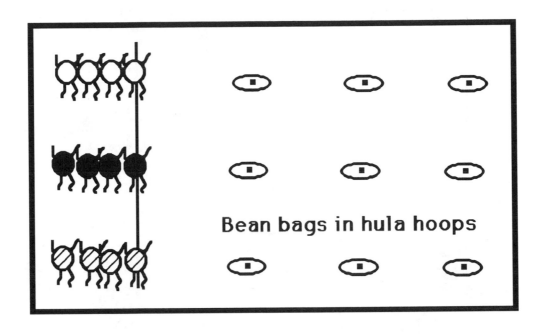

Bean bags in hula hoops

Age Appeal: Kindergarten and Up   **Also good for teens and adults**

Purpose: Cardiovascular fitness and teamwork skills

Equipment: Hula hoops and beanbags

Group Size: Any size

Setting: Gym or outdoors

DESCRIPTION: Divide the class into groups of 3-4 players. Opposite each team are three hula hoops spaced out about 10 feet apart. A beanbag is placed in each hoop. On the command to start, the first players in each line run to the first hula hoops, grab the beanbag, and carry them back to the starting line. The beanbags are placed on the starting line. The same players now run to the second hula hoops, take the beanbag from the hoops, and carry them to the starting line. This continues until all three beanbags are on the starting line. The first runner tags the next player.

The next player takes one of the beanbags from the starting line and places it in the first hula hoop. He gets another beanbag and places it in the second hula hoop. This continues until all of the beanbags have been replaced into the three hoops. The relay continues with the next player taking the beanbags out of the hoops. When the last player finishes, all of the players on the team run to the far hula hoop, place one foot in the hoop and yell "Hoopla!"

Roll and Run Relay

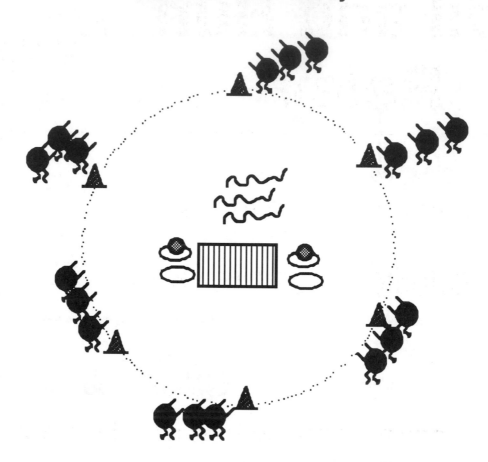

Age Appeal: Third Grade and Up　　　**Also good for teens**

Purpose: Cardiovascular fitness, teamwork, and sport skills

Equipment: Dice, jump ropes, balls, hula hoops, cones, mats

Group Size: Any size

Setting: Gym or outdoors

DESCRIPTION: Divide the class into groups of 3-4 players. The teams are assembled equal distance from the needed equipment which is placed in the center of the activity area. Each team has a die. A large poster board displays the six different tasks. To play, a starting signal is given and the first players in each line roll the die.

The number rolled determines the task this player must perform. After rolling the die, the student goes to the center area, selects the appropriate equipment, and performs the task. Upon completion, the student runs one lap around the circle and tags the next player. This continues until all players have completed two turns. A sample list of tasks can be found on the next page.

Roll and Run Relay

#1   Jump rope ten times.

#2   Dribble the ball 15 times.

#3   Do 5 curl-ups on the mat.

#4   Shake hands with eight different people not on your team.

#5   Stand on one leg and yell "I love physical education!"

#6   Step inside the hula hoop and pull it up (from feet to head) and off the top of your head two times.

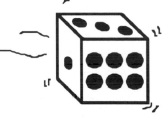

Memory Task Relay

Age Appeal: Third Grade and Up   **Also good for teens**

Purpose: Teamwork, sequencing and memory skills

Equipment: None

Group Size: Any size

Setting: Gym or outdoors

DESCRIPTION: Divide the class into groups of 3-4 players. The teams assemble behind a starting line. The teacher will read a short set of tasks. The object of this relay is for the first player to listen to the tasks and perform them in the correct sequence. For example:

> 1.) Run to the opposite wall and back,
>
> 2.) Crawl under the legs of your teammates,
>
> 3.) Form a circle and hold hands with your teammates as everyone sits down and stands back up while holding hands.
>
> 4.) Tag the next player!

The number of specific tasks requested will vary from grade to grade. Younger students will be comfortable with 2-3 simple tasks, while the older students may be able to handle 4-7 tasks. Keeping score is not as important to the students as their ability to complete the task as a team. When all of the players have had a turn, give the students a new set of directions for the next relay. Here are two more sets of sample relay tasks:

1.) Slide two times to your right,
2.) Jump as far as possible in any direction,
3.) Run one time around your teammates,
4.) Touch all four walls of the gym,
5.) Tag the next player!

1.) Jump as high in the air as you can,
2.) Run and touch any two walls of the gym (your choice),
3.) Skip to the basketball court center circle and run back,
4.) "High five" all of your teammates,
5.) Tag the next player!

Long Long Jump Relay

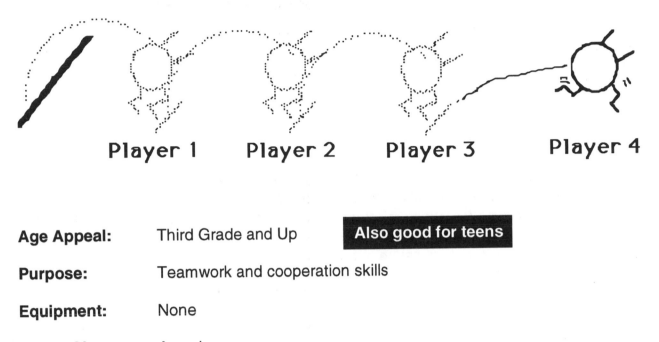

Player 1   **Player 2**   **Player 3**   **Player 4**

Age Appeal: Third Grade and Up   Also good for teens

Purpose: Teamwork and cooperation skills

Equipment: None

Group Size: Any size

Setting: Gym or outdoors

DESCRIPTION: Divide the class into teams of 3-4 players. The first jumper from each team begins behind the starting line. The object of this relay is to see how far the team can jump collectively. Team members take turns jumping. The second person jumps from the spot where the first jumper landed. A variety of jumps can be used, one type for each round. For example, in the first round the students use a standing broad jump. In the second round, the students do a running broad jump. In the third round, the students do a standing one-foot hop, etc. In every case, each player's jump begins where the last one ended.

Variations:	• The team members count the number of jumps it takes for them to cover a certain distance. The object is to see how many total jumps are required to travel from a starting line to a finishing line.
	• Each jump is actually measured with a measuring tape. Team members record and then total the collective distance. The team with the greatest distance wins.
	• Teams try to improve their collective distances with additional rounds. They compete against themselves, rather than against other teams.

Discipline Tip #8: Everyone Wins

As we all know, dealing with youngsters is a complicated endeavor. Here are more student management tips that have proved useful for teachers and youth leaders.

Who is Keeping Score? Another interesting "problem preventer" is making changes in the way you keep score for games and other activities. There may be situations where the emphasis on winning is causing friction between team or individual players. Here are a few suggestions for dealing with this problem:

- Don't keep or post the scores.
- Change the makeup of the teams often.
- Use outlandish scores: 100 points for making a basket or goal.
- Change the scoring system. How about a score of "10 pigs and 3 sheep"?
- Don't call out the scores or recognize winners. "If you had fun, you won!"

Be Sociable: One interesting way to cut down on potential problems is to let your students know you are interested in them as a person. Planning an after-school social event for your students and/or parents provides another opportunity for you to get to know them on a different level. As a physical education teacher, youth leader, or recreational specialist, you will probably have your share of opportunities to be involved in planning a variety of social events. Here are a few suggestions for making this event a successful one!

1. **Be Ready!** Hosts and hostesses should be ready to meet and greet guests at least 15 to 20 minutes prior to the actual announced starting time.

2. **The Party Begins When the First Guests Arrive!** The party begins when the first guests arrive. Pre-party games or activities should begin at once.

3. **Play Background Music!** Appropriate, lively music should be playing.

4. **Keep It Short!** Pre-party activities should continue no longer than 20 minutes after the announced starting time. Participants arriving late will just not finish.

5. **Recognize the Participants!** If any of the pre-party activities involves a contest (see how many of something can be found or collected), use the first "whole group" activity to recognize the "winners."

7 Parachute Games:
"Uplifting Activities for All!"

Nothing excites a group like playing with a parachute! Just maneuvering the parachute (moving it up and down, shaking it, crawling over and under it, etc.) is a lot of fun and a great physical workout.

About Parachutes: It is a good idea, when first introducing parachute play, not to engage the group in a game situation until they have first had an opportunity to experiment and "just play around with it." Parachute play records and tapes are available with suitable musical accompaniment and verbal directions provided, and these may be helpful to a teacher or leader, but are unnecessary for success. Parachutes, in addition to being equipment for games and activities, are ideal for other uses:

- Ground cover for seating

- Draped for acoustical assistance

- Draped for stage covering or backdrop

- Decorations

Parachute Pointers: Here are a few "care and feeding" tips to get maximum use of your parachute.

- If the parachute is too big or too heavy for the group to lift successfully, gather the material into the hands of participants, making the parachute small enough to handle.

- To successfully "fold" the parachute for storing: Participants can roll and gather material into the center or you can grasp the center of the parachute and twirl it over and over until it is wound.

- If storing in a bag or container, be sure parachute is dry. The parachute can be washed in a washing machine if it gets too dirty.

Toss Up!

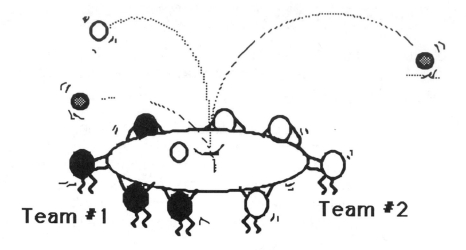

Team #1   Team #2

Age Appeal:	Third Grade and Up	**Also good for teens and adults**
Purpose:	Cooperation and teamwork skills	
Equipment:	One parachute and four large foam balls (two of each color)	
Group Size:	Any size	
Setting:	Gym or outdoors	

DESCRIPTION: The players hold onto a parachute with both hands, facing inward. Players are then divided into two teams. Four large foam balls, two of each color, are placed on top of the parachute. Each team claims the balls of one color.

The object of the game is for a team to flip and shake the parachute so that balls belonging to the opponent are bounced over the heads of players and off the parachute. And, at the same time, each team tries to prevent their balls from bouncing off. The teacher gives the signal to begin, and play continues until both balls of one team have been bounced off.

Teacher Tips: Remind the players not to touch the balls with their hands. Players may not lower the parachute to allow the balls to roll off. A ball must exit over the heads of the players.

Ball Exchange

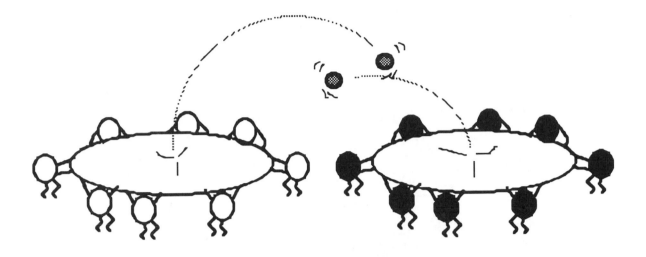

Age Appeal: Fourth Grade and Up   **Also good for teens and adults**

Purpose: Cooperation and teamwork skills

Equipment: Two parachutes and two playground balls

Group Size: Any size

Setting: Gym or outdoors

DESCRIPTION: The participants are divided into two groups and each group holds onto a parachute. Groups are spaced about 6 feet apart. One group has a ball (playground ball or volleyball) that is placed in the center of their parachute.

On a signal to begin, the group with the ball works together to try to lift and propel the ball so it can be caught in the other group's parachute. The group with the second parachute will also have to work together as they learn to move to meet the oncoming ball.

Each group should have numerous opportunities to catch and throw the ball. After the groups have become proficient, challenge them to a dual exchange. In a dual exchange, both groups have a ball. Both groups will throw simultaneously and catch the other group's ball!

Parachute Exchange

Age Appeal: Fourth Grade and Up   **Also good for teens and adults**

Purpose: Cooperation and teamwork skills

Equipment: Two parachutes and two cones

Group Size: Any size

Setting: Gym or outdoors

DESCRIPTION: This fun game is played with two parachutes. Each team stands spaced around a parachute with members holding on with one or both hands. A parachute is centered over a traffic cone or circle drawn on the ground.

On a signal "go," teams attempt to beat the others by moving from their original traffic cone to another cone trading places in the shortest possible time. Players must all continue to hold on to the parachute throughout the move and the cone should be directly under the center of the parachute for a successful finish.

Teacher Tip: Teamwork is essential for success. Doing several rounds of this game will help the players improve!

Overtake

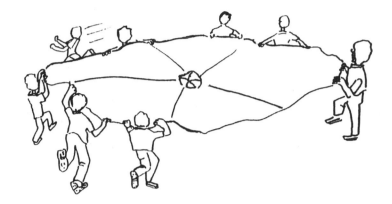

Age Appeal: Second Grade and Up   **Also good for teens and adults**

Purpose: Cardiovascular fitness

Equipment: One parachute

Group Size: Any size

Setting: Gym or outdoors

DESCRIPTION: The participants all face one direction and hold on to the parachute with the hand closest to it. All participants number off 1-4. The teacher calls out a traveling locomotive movement (slow jog, skip, fast walk, etc.) and everyone begins to circle around using that locomotor skill.

The teacher then calls out one of the numbers. Participants with that number let go of the parachute and quickly run around the group in the same direction to return to their original places. Play continues as a different locomotive movement and a new number are called.

Teacher Tip: This activity is aerobically challenging, so short rest periods might be necessary. The group's locomotive movements should be kept slow-paced.

Pick 'Em Up

Age Appeal: Second Grade and Up   **Also good for teens and adults**

Purpose: General fitness and teamwork skills

Equipment: One parachute, two plastic buckets, numerous small balls, and a stopwatch

Group Size: Any size

Setting: Gym or outdoors

DESCRIPTION: About 2 dozen small, lightweight balls are placed on top of a parachute. Two players, equipped with a container large enough to hold the balls, also get on top of the parachute. To play, all of the other players grasp the edges of the parachute and shake the parachute up and down. The two players on top compete to see which one can collect the most balls in their container. When all balls have been collected, they are counted and the winner chooses two other players to compete.

Teacher Tips:
- The players on the parachute should catch the balls with the buckets while they are in the air without handling them.
- Continual shaking of the parachute is tiring, so time should be short (about 1-2 minutes) for catching.

166

The Giant Popcorn Machine

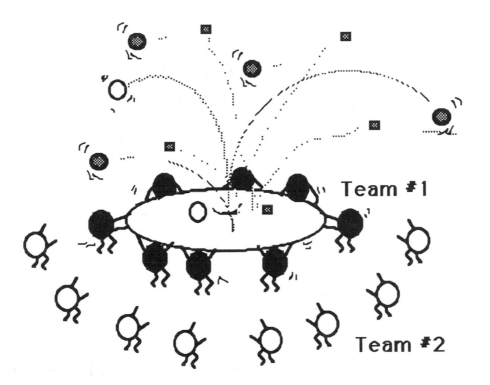

Age Appeal: Kindergarten and Up

Purpose: General fitness and teamwork skills

Equipment: One parachute, numerous balls and beanbags, and a stopwatch

Group Size: Any size

Setting: Gym or outdoors

DESCRIPTION: Players are divided into two teams. About 2-4 dozen small balls and/or beanbags are placed on top of a parachute. Players of one team space themselves around the parachute and hold on with both hands.

On a signal "go," players shake the parachute and try to bounce the balls off in as short a time as possible (usually this takes about a minute). Balls must bounce off, not roll off. Then, players of a second team take their places around the parachute, balls are again placed on top, and this group tries to bounce the balls off in a shorter period of time.

Rotate the Number

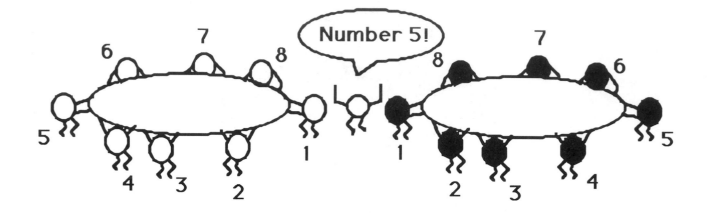

Age Appeal: Kindergarten and Up

Purpose: General fitness and teamwork skills

Equipment: Two parachutes and two wooden wands

Group Size: Any size

Setting: Gym or outdoors

DESCRIPTION: The participants are divided into two equal teams. Each team encircles one of the parachutes, which are spaced on either side of the leader. Players hold on to the edge of the parachute and number off. The leader, standing between the two teams, extends his arms out to the sides in the direction of each team. A wooden wand (or other suitable object) is held in each hand.

To play, the leader calls out one of the numbers. Without letting go of the parachute, players must circulate so that the person with the number that was called can grab the wand from the leader's hand. The object is for a team to be first to grab a wand from the leader's hand. One point is earned for doing this.

Play continues for 5-10 minutes, as the leader continues to call out numbers. The teams circle in one direction, and then the other, to grab the wand first.

Teacher Tips: • Remind the players not to lean across their parachute or let go of it.

        • Circles of rope can be substituted for the parachutes.

Trading Places

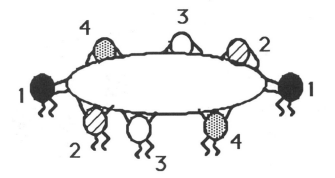

Age Appeal: Second Grade and Up   `Also good for teens and adults`

Purpose: Cooperation and teamwork skills

Equipment: One parachute

Group Size: Any size

Setting: Gym or outdoors

DESCRIPTION: This low organizational activity is a good one to start with after your group has become familiar with handling the parachute. All participants stand holding the parachute with both hands, facing inward. They number off so that there are two to four players with the same number. For example: If there are 20 players, you will have the students number off by 1-4, 1-5, or 1-10.

To begin, the group lifts the parachute in unison. At the height of the lift, the leader calls out a number (or numbers). Players with that number must leave their spot and travel under the parachute to a place vacated by another player with that same number. Players are safe if they find a new spot before the parachute drops down to touch them.

Teacher Tips: • To give more dimension to the game, vary the locomotive movements for traveling.

• Require players to travel with their "bumpers up" (hands up and out in front) for safety purposes.

Reach High Today!

Author Unknown

No one reaching for the stars ever comes up with a handful of mud.

Reaching high keeps a person on his toes!

Yesterday is history.

Tomorrow is a mystery.

But today is a gift.

That's why it's called the "present."